T0197354

EPSILONS
and
DELTAS
of
Life

EVERYDAY
STORIES,
VOLUME I

SATISH C. BHATNAGAR

Books by the same Author

Scattered Matherticles: Mathematical Reflections, Volume I (2010)
Vectors in History: Main Foci—India and USA, Volume 1 (2012)

Order this book online at www.trafford.com
or email orders@trafford.com

Most Trafford titles are also available at major online book retailers.

Printed in the United States of America.

ISBN: 978-1-4669-3427-6 (sc)
ISBN: 978-1-4669-3428-3 (e)

Trafford rev. 06/05/2012

 www.trafford.com

North America & international
toll-free: 1 888 232 4444 (USA & Canada)
phone: 250 383 6864 ♦ fax: 812 355 4082

ABBREVIATED READERS' COMMENTS

I HAVEN'T been back to India for 11 years. I have been wanting to; but your walking episode discourages me even more. **Baldev Singh**/Yuba City, CA

You are inspiring me to start writing . . . **Harpreet Singh**/Silicon Valley, CA

Hi Dr. Bhatnagar, I never would have guessed that this side of you exists! Your writing is fresh and brings a great deal to life, despite the topic. I will forward a more detailed response on Tuesday. Take care, **Renato**

What was your enlightenment? Actually seeing misery in hospital makes one a bigger philosopher than a whole day in place of worship. Watching cremation or burial gives one bigger lesson in spirituality than a day of meditation. **Rahul**/Austin, TX

I am enjoying your discoveries. It is very interesting to read what you have to offer. **Matt.**

I read both of your recent Reflections together and was surprised how a person of your stature can shuttle from abysmal to buoyant. However, the Flight *wala* is amusing and reflects how you can make best use of whatever you have and not only this you make it intellectually stimulating as well. I don't know whether I am intellectually fit or mature enough to comment on your reflections, however I wanted to do it. Please do always keep me on your mailing list. **Jagjeet**

Subba Rao Bhai Ji is a Great courageous and thoughtful soul! It is difficult to find such living enlightened saints. He really deserves the honor of Nobel Prize. **Sundrani**

Bad English is bad English! It is no excuse for creativity! Dr. A. R. **Bhatia**

Maybe you should have worshipped "Maxy". Hindus also worship their gods. I don't see how you can compare communication with god to talking to a car! One is worship and belief and the other is simply eccentricity. And yes it was a fine machine—your car. Will need some work on the suspension soon though. **Anir.**

Your letters wake me up about different aspects of our life and society. Thank you for adding me on your E-Mail list. **Atul Majmudar**

Bhatnagar Sahib: Mathematics and Philosophy are not that far apart after all. I think many people think and feel the way you do but they do not give expression to these emotions. Some time it is even scary to think openly about these issues. This was a well-written and thought out piece, **Ved P. Sharma**

Very apt observations. To remain as optimistic as possible, try to philosophize on what others have which we are not fortunate enough, realizing that no one has it all, be grateful for what we do have . . . . in short contentment and a dedication to some cause beyond our personal life is the key to happiness. Very human to forget!! Regards. **RAJA**

EPSILONS AND DELTAS OF LIFE: EVERYDAY STORIES, VOLUME I

DEDICATED TO

Ishwar Chandra
(1937 -)

SATISH C. BHATNAGAR

ON A SPECIAL TITLE

Titles of the books are very important to me—like that of a typical woman picking a dress for her wardrobe for an evening function. It takes several weeks for finalization. I involved my students and colleagues by writing a following *Mathematical Reflection* on the title alone:

"Last week, I asked my students, in *Discrete Mathematics I* and *Calculus III* courses—about what is conveyed by the phrase—*'epsilons and deltas of life'*. They simply demurred. A few of them said that they had heard of epsilon and delta in the definition of Limit in a previous calculus course. Yes, that is where I too encountered them first. It was in 1957, in my third year of college—55 years ago! The English letters, 'e/E' and 'd/D' correspond to epsilon, ε / E and delta, δ / Δ. Linguistically speaking, they are the 5th and 4th letters in their respective languages. This linguist correlation is historical, as English may be the second or third derivative of Greek and Latin languages via the Roman occupation of Greece in the 3rd century BC.

"I told my students that, as a latter-day writer, I love to coin new words and create new phrases. It is an extension of doing any research. In fact, a creative work is bound to spill over into other walks of life. It is in this spirit, a new phrase, *epsilons and deltas of life*, is being introduced. It will eventually find a place in the lexicon. Its usage reminds me of the current draw on Mexican 'salsa' for anything, hot & sexy and 'enchilada' in communicating something like 'a whole thing'. They were not heard of 20 years ago.

"This phrase is intended to capture what is conveyed by *'The Nitties—Gritties of life'*, *'Nuts and Bolts of Life'*, *'Commas and Periods of Life'*. As a matter of fact, each one of them was considered as the title of my third book at different stages of its compilation. But they lost to *'Epsilons and Deltas of Life'*. Reason is obvious—it alone sounds mathematical! One may say—why to be hung up on mathematical—for selling a book?

"Fifty plus years ago, I chose college teaching of mathematics as my profession. I was in India then. Often, I am asked questions on this choice—like 'do you like/love it?' My response is like this: "If you have been in a relationship with a person, place or principle for over 30 years, then either you are in love with it, or have faked a chunk of life away"!

"In fact, I go a step further. After 40-50 years in a profession, it cuts deep grooves into the psyche. With awareness, it can become a window of life—a paradigm. That is what mathematics means to me now. It broke out 20 years ago, when I first offered an honors seminar, *Mathematical Thinking in Liberal Arts*—exploring bridges with music, visual arts, humanities and law. This seminar was offered there times. It has intellectually emboldened me.

"I ran a small survey on this phrase. It made little sense to people in India. In the US, April is a month of mathematical awareness. Public is either in awe or appreciation for math. The phrase is well received, though it may not be fully understood. It is an extension of American love for ethnic foods, music, apparels, travels—and what not. Last night, I told a friend in India that this won't be the title of an Indian edition of this book. Realistically speaking, what good a gourmet food is, if it is not enjoyed by anyone? A book is not a journal. I have written it for public consumption intended to last for a long time!"

(April 13, 2012)

ABOUT THE FRONT COVER OF THE BOOK

This is the first time that I decided to write a ***Reflection*** on the designing of my third book. The front cover of the first book was put together by my son and 'daughternal' granddaughter. As for the second book, it was hurriedly designed by me with the help of Trafford's art department. It is well received. This time, I enjoyed designing the cover for the third book. In brief, dominant white color, with sporadic snowflake bluish tinges in it, captures the essence of philosophy and characteristics of philosophers. The pictures of Pythagoras, Bertrand Russell and Hardayal Mathur are very much personal to me!

Pythagoras (570-495 BC) is the one of the four immortal polymaths of ancient Greece. The other three are: Socrates (469-399 BC), Plato (428-348 BC) and Aristotle (384-324 BC). A word is called for Archimedes (287-212 BC) too, who is considered as all time great mathematician, scientist, engineer, and inventor. Only Isaac Newton comes close to him. They all have influenced me in varying degrees. Pythagoras truly set an intellectual tradition rolling in by combining the study of mathematics, philosophy, metaphysics and natural sciences. On a small scale, it has turned out to be a story of my life too.

Pythagoras' music of the sphere, his Theorem and Golden Ratio stand out in the minds of any thinking person. He is equally known for founding an academy named after him. Pythagoreans had divine belief in natural numbers that they explain the secrets of nature. The members took an oath of secrecy to its beliefs. Eventfully, it proved that the excess of everything is bad—when the existence of irrational numbers forced its one member, Hippasus of Metapontum to commit suicide, be drowned, or murdered. The Academy survived several centuries, though, this incident happened 100 years after its founding.

It must be added that Euclid (323-283 BC) was all mathematics—his genius was to lay the axiomatic foundations of geometry. ***The Elements***, Euclid's magnum opus, became a benchmark of mathematical rigor for centuries to come. Anyway, Pythagoras remains as the earliest great mind of Greek antiquity. Incidentally, he was a contemporary of Confucius (551-479 BC) in China and Buddha (563-463 BC) in India.

I tried to connect myself with an Indian mind of antiquity, but there is no trace of anyone! Indian heritage went through so many upheavals due to the subjugation of the Hindus by various Muslim rulers and European colonizers that only shreds of evidence exist before 500 AD. It is a monumental task to re-create a history of India going back to 600 BC, when minds, like Buddha, flourished in India. **Foreign subjugation robs a nation not only of its resources but also of its heritage.** Scattered evidence of mathematics and sciences, as found in the Vedas, indicate that great minds did thrive in the BC era.

The name of Bertrand Russell (1872-1970) was on the lips of college kids in India of the 1950s. His essays were included in every anthology used in English courses required for all four years. I still remember Russell's line in an essay: fools build the houses and wise live in them. Years later, I realized and practiced its merits—like, it frees the young to pursue opportunities in different lands without encumbrances of home ownership.

Galib, a nickname of Madan Lal Garg, my college friend, was an avid fan of Russell, and we often talked about Russell's writings. Russell influenced me on many fronts—as the greatest mathematical logician of his decade, a prolific writer of par excellence, a world teacher, man of convictions, and renowned pacifist in the last two decades of his life. In 1968, I devoured his three-volume autobiography. He wrote the third volume two years before his death, at age 97. His spans of longevity and productivity are equal!

From his autobiography, his relationships with women stand out in my mind. Each occasion of divorcing a wife coincided with a cusp in his intellectual development. Throughout life, he was rumored to have liaisons with the women of high society into which he was born in and grew up around. His controversial stands acted as magnets!

Russell would have won the Fields Medal in 1920 for his seminal work in mathematical logic—leading up to 3-volume, *Principia of Mathematica* (1910-1913). But the medal was instituted in 1936! However, he won the 1950 Nobel Prize for Literature, and missed getting the Nobel for Peace! During the 20th century, no other intellectual was more recognized in every continent and in every nation to the extent as Bertrand Russell was.

Not surprisingly, Russell's essays and my *Reflections* have some intersection. Both are centered around an immediate incident—be that physical, mental, or social. Often, there is an element of provocation to the readers to think anew. His essays on marriage and morals, written after his US visit, became classic—pieces of originality and boldness of his mind. For his social and political stands, he was often at odds with the UK and US governments. He was an ultimate non-conformist.

Hardayal Mathur's impact on my life runs deep, wide and long. He is popularly known as Lala Hardayal (Lala is honorific title). For putting him in relative perspective, let me go back to the other two. Pythagoras is an all time intellectual mind that no literate person can escape his influence. Russell's dominance of 20th century's total landscape of intellectual, social, political and philosophical was so pervasive, that no sensitive person was easily spared of his influence. The story of Hardayal's influence on me begins from my home. Bhatnagars and Mathurs being members of the Kayastha community, his name was on the lips of every family member. Kids were told of his phenomenon memory and securing first class first distinction in every exam. It inspired me for academic success.

However, no elder ever told me of his political activities, his exile from India and banishment from India. His book, *Hints for Self Culture* (1934), banned in British India, remains very popular. I first read it in 1962 and liked it so much that I used to gift it away on weddings and birthday celebrations etc. Any idea or person, liked in youthful years of life, continues to sprout later in its different phases.

My diverse intellectual interests are traceable to Hardayal. Much later, I understood that his book was like a manifesto for the making of new generations of Indian intellectuals so that they could understand their political subjugation and fight for liberation. Anyone reading it is awed by the 'giantness' of his mind and calls for action.

In the history of India, most Kayasthas served their Muslim and British masters in high administrative positions. It goes back to nearly 500 years. When my historic awareness broadened, I was, at times, ashamed and embarrassed of the roles of my ancestors.

However, Hardayal is a rare exception, and he exponentially rose in my esteem. During his stay in the US, he taught in Stanford University, organized Indians, and founded the Gadar Party in San Francisco for the liberation of India. Even at this point of my life at 70+, Hardayal continues to inspire me with his benchmarks in scholarship, leadership and social activities.

April 29, 2012

PS

About my picture on the back cover: The photo for the first book was taken in a Bathinda photo studio, the second one by my younger daughter Annie, and the third one by my niece, Shweta.

TIME FOR A PHILOSOPHIC PREFACE

My first book contains *Mathematical Reflections,* and the second one is a compilation of *Reflections* that are historical in nature. The next choice was sequentially simple—it is to bring out the first volume of my *Reflections* that comprises philosophical types.

First: What is Philosophy? To the best of my knowledge, philosophizing an act or thought is inherently unique to human beings only. Unlike sensory delights that are easily understood, philosophization may be construed as a pleasure of intellect for leisurely few.

At the age of 70+, I have developed relatively a pragmatic point of view of philosophy. For me, **philosophy is a distillation of experiences**. This distillation is an infinite extension of *fractional distillation*, a chemical process for separating particular compounds from a mixture at increasingly higher temperatures corresponding to their boiling points. This technique fascinated me so much at the age of 17 that it became embedded in my consciousness. It is a joy to apply this technique in life—viewed as a mixture of experiences. With maturity of mind, one can bring them out to tackle life problems and extract gems of thoughts.

Pure vs. Applied: Yes, like mathematics, popularly divided into pure math and applied math, philosophy too has its share of such a division—pure and applied. Every young initiate is sucked into this controversy. My understanding tells that anything understood purely pure eventually finds a utilitarian attribute, and thus turns into applied. In my mind, applied philosophy goes off from a routine scenario, but the pure one stems out from the assumptions of esoteric concepts.

Where are my philosophical moorings? This question has to be addressed thoroughly. First of all, a Hindu mind is essentially philosophical—irrespective of profession, education and age. By and large, it is passive when it comes to taking actions in life. This characteristic is also due to some historical realities related to the last millennium. Aside from that, look at the number of Hindu scriptures—the four holy *Vedas* contain more matter than the scriptures of all other religions combined.

In India, kids and adults are routinely observed engaging in informal philosophical and religious discussions. During my college days (1955-59), incidental study of Swami Ram Tirath's volumes (1873-1906), ***In the Woods of God Realization***, had a formative influence on my mind. Swami is an honorific title of a male Hindu monk and ascetic. Incidentally, Ram Tirath was first rate mathematics student and professor, but he quit the profession for a monastic order after a chance meeting with Swami Vivekananda (1863-1902). During the years, 1902-04, he also preached Hindu philosophy in the US.

Traditional Hindu society is super ritualistic. But I grew up in a reasonably non-ritualistic family and in an open atmosphere of Arya Samaj advocating formlessness of God. Arya Samaj is a Hindu renaissance movement started in 1875 by Swami Dayanand (1824-1883). In every culture, rituals of an organized religion, theology and philosophy are all integrated. However, lately in the US—God, religious rituals and theology are not a part of the academic circles of philosophy and psychology. Consequently, any discussion of ethics and morality ends up dry and shallow.

While growing up in India, frequent meetings with my celibate maternal uncle, Swami Deekshanand (1920-2003), a renowned leader of Arya Samaj, pushed my thoughts towards a broader philosophy of life. After my settling down in the US, spending a week with him during India visits, used to be a highlight of my trip. A book on his life is on my agenda of publications.

Something very tangible happened in the fall of 1961. Himmat Singh Sinha, a philosophy lecturer and my colleague in Government Rajindra College, Bathinda, introduced me to the pleasures of philosophy of science at a time when I was studying Einstein's Theory Relativity on my own. It was a kind of revelation, as to how the cutting edges of science become philosophical inquiries naturally. It is weird in a sense that one does not have to have technical knowledge of the sciences to become a student of philosophy of science!

Another milestone in the study of philosophy came during 1965-67 when I started my PhD (unfinished) in Mathematical Seismology in Kurukshetra University (KU), Kurukshetra. At the same time, my wife, a month after the birth of our first-born daughter, started her MA in philosophy from Punjabi University, Patiala. All the textbooks and notes needed for her courses were checked out from KU library or borrowed from Himmat Singh Sinha and his friends. The graduate textbooks, being written by foreign authors, were very expensive in India throughout the 1960s. For example, a particular math textbook was priced at half of my father's monthly salary!

Every 2-3 weeks, I used to undertake a 3-hour train journey between Kurukshetra and Patiala, for family reasons and taking out, or bringing back philosophy textbooks. It was during these trips that I would browse them, and sometimes read them aloud to my wife. Our infant daughter demanded attention too! To make it short, philosophy gradually seeped into my thoughts, studies and writings. Amongst a few corollaries, I am a charter member of SIGPOM (Special Interest Group Philosophy Of Mathematics) of MAA (Mathematical Association of America).

The schools of philosophy, whether eastern and western, are not my cup of tea. Moreover, any claim of originality on a philosophical thought is very different from an industrial patent, a mathematics theorem, or a scientific principle. No one can truly claim ownership of a so-called philosophical doctrine. I may not be able to delineate a school of philosophy, but can confidently expound upon it. The western philosophical thoughts, relative to the eastern ones, are far more grounded in social, political and economical conditions.

My philosophical excursions took a quantum leap during my KU stay when I first read the books of J. Krishnamurti (1895-1982). Rajneesh/Osho (1929-90) appeared like a meteor in the firmament of the sky. Galib, a close friend of 55 years, introduced me to Rajneesh's thoughts and oratory during my 1975 visit to India—the first after an absence of seven years. In a nutshell, Rajneesh's philosophical expositions feel like a drink of quality scotch. Krishnamurti can be described as an ultimate pure philosopher, and Osho as a consummate applied philosopher, or mystic. They have enriched my thoughts. No matter what, with this philosophical armor, I feel very confident about venturing into newer horizons of life! However, for me, philosophical flights always remain subservient to the deductive reasoning of mathematics.

What is my Philosophy? A long-time friend and retired English professor asked me to explain my philosophy in this Preface too. It is a good suggestion. When analyzed, then it really raised more questions. **Is it a philosophy of my life?** I have explained what philosophy means to me. Philosophy of life has to be different from the objectives and missions in life, as they are functions of years in age. What I used to think of life in my 20s has little to do with my pool of thoughts at the age of 72 years now.

Philosophy of life may be viewed as being closer to the approaches towards various aspects of life. For instance, I have written on philosophy of my teaching. And this question can be applied to any activity. Nevertheless, philosophy does go beyond technicality of an approach—integrating ethics, morality and vision into its transcendent nature. And whatever is my philosophy, it really comes out through ninety-two *Reflections* included in this book. Needless to say, philosophy is also tied with insightfulness in any routine of life.

What are the contents of this book? Let me say at the outset that the contents do not look like any passages from philosophy textbooks. On the contrary, every reader will be able to identify with some scenario that prompted me to write that particular *Reflection*. The subtitle of the book, *EVERYDAY STORIES* says in all. Invariably, a reader would say it to himself or herself, "I know it, I have thought of it, I could write it too, etc". Yes, it is at that very moment, I take the reader to a new level of delight and understanding. That is my forte—making an ordinary situation look extraordinary.

For some convenience, ninety-two *Reflections,* written through the year 2008, are divided into three general sections. By the very nature of reflective writing, the sections are no way mutually disjoint. A typical *Reflection* traverses multiple themes. The headings of the sections are: **INTERPERSONAL, SOCIO-POLITICAL,** and **MUNDANE.** Also, their respective mathematical headings, in parentheses, are **LOCAL, INTERVAL** and **GLOBAL.** They are taken from mathematical concepts. A property is **local** if it is defined at individual points only –such as, '**Limit** of a function at a point'. However, '**Integration** of a function' is defined over an **interval**. A property is **global** when it is true at every point, say, on a line, plane, or space. These are my favorite classifications and I try to fit them in as many settings as possible in life.

Is there any order in Reflections? Not really—as the *Reflections* are written in different times, spaces, and moods. The only thing I increasingly believe is the date on which a *Reflection* was started on. For me, it is very important to know the date, when a certain idea originated. It indicates the evolution of a writer's mind. When I read the works of a so-called great mind, I want to pitch my writings up front. And without any information of time period, fair comparisons are not possible. To drive home this point, at age 20, I could connect two points in life if they were 10 units apart, but now I can span two points over 1000 units apart. In other words, I have been out-thinking many minds that I was in awe of during my youthful years.

Unique Features of the Book: In the literary world, dominated by poetry and fiction, my reflecting writing is absolutely grounded in non-fiction. Nevertheless, it takes the readers to stratospheric heights. Another feature is space for personal notes. Being a compulsive writer of pencil notes in the margins, tops and bottoms of the pages of a book, I feel constrained for lack of sufficient space. There is a mathematical correlation: the number of notations made in a book is directly proportional to reader's maturity of mind. That is why I have provided some space after every 7-8 *Reflections*.

As in the previous two books, there is no **Index** at the end. Reason, any topic may be touched in a dozen of *Reflections*. Since the *Reflections* are self-contained, a **bibliography** has no place either. Lately, I have started disliking bibliography, as it often pads a small substantial material. It also amounts to paddling a line of thought to a certain degree! On the other hand, I have continued a new tradition of thumbnail sketches of some commentators at the end. Finally, each *Reflection* is almost independent of one before it and one after it. Thus, one can browse the book from any *Reflection* and digest it easily.

Dedication: This book is dedicated to my friend Ishwar Chandra whom I first met in Ambala Cantt 22 years ago. As an erstwhile publisher, editor, writer, and printer, he understands all the nuances of the industry—from writings to finished publications. It was the beauty of his small pamphlet that got us acquainted a year before we met face to face. He is incredible in demanding perfection in writing. He convinced me to go back to my *Reflections* again and again—like a goldsmith working on a piece of jewelry ordered for a queen. It is the result of this kind of exercises that reflective writing has become for me a medium of self-realization.

Acknowledgements: Finally, I thank my numerous e-readers across the world, who, over the years, have provided occasional feedback. Now, we are cyber companions in an exploration of life. However, I must single out Francis Andrew, a Scotsman and professor of English, for helping me re-learn the syntax of the English language. I met him in Jan 2009 in Nizwa, Oman during my one semester visiting assignment at the University of Nizwa. Since then, he has suggested improvements in each and every *Reflection*. So much so that I have yet to write an 'error free' *Reflection*!

In conclusion, any feedback and comments on any aspect of the book, e-mailed at <u>bhatnaga@unlv.nevada.edu</u>, would be thankfully acknowledged.

Satish C. Bhatnagar
May 02, 2012

DISTRIBUTION OF CONTENTS

I.   INTERPERSONAL SCENARIOS (Local)

A DAY OF LIFE IN USA

Yesterday was quite a day. In the morning, I visited Desert Rose High School for adults—located in a predominantly poor section of Las Vegas. This visit was part of a **PAYBAC** Program (acronym for *Professionals And Youth Building A Commitment*) of the school district in which individuals and company representatives from various walks of life volunteer their time to motivate the students by telling their personal stories of success. During a welcome gathering, before going to the classrooms, the lady principal of the school described the administration of the school and its student body.

The school essentially remains open from 8 AM to 8 PM. Students attend classes around their jobs and family responsibilities. Most teachers are part time employees—from active in other jobs to the retired ones. The age of the students varies from 17 years to 70+. She remarked how sometimes an entire family takes courses at different hours, but they may graduate together. There are lots of students whose first language is not English.

Talking of family backgrounds, the principal described a student, a 17-year-old girl with three children 3, 2, and 1 year old. No questions are asked! While children are looked after by grandparents, the mother attends school. Persons with such life styles are likely to be lost in the shuffles of life in most countries of the world—including some European. **It is in the US alone where opportunities are made available that one has the best chances to actualize one's potential**. It is a state school. People grudgingly pay taxes, but they value human growth through education.

In the evening, I was a guest in a crowd of nearly 500 people gathered in a hall of the Alexis Hotel, an upscale all suite non-gambling hotel. It was a graduation of ceremony for nearly 150 persons, who had completed **four day, 36 hour** seminars in the previous week. My wife was one of them. The seminars are called **PSI Seminars** (acronym for *People Synergistically Involved*). The fee is $450 with money back guarantee, if not satisfied. Also, once paid, one can attend the same seminar any number of times. In an hour-long program, the felicitator of the organization gave a well-orchestrated speech rather a histrionic performance.

After the new graduates were recognized on the stage, the felicitator used them to highlight the seminars in developing physical, behavioral, emotional and spiritual sides of personality. He did not tell the audience what exactly is done during seminars, as secrecy enhances curiosity. However, he did convince some guests and family members that they rushed to register for the next seminars. The speaker was dynamic, confident, and exuded a charisma of a successful person.

The thrust of these seminars is to develop the right attitudes. According to a Harvard study, success in life essentially depends on right attitudes; skills are secondary and knowledge counts only 10-20 %. There are no age limits, educational minimum, or other filters for taking these seminars. This was a bit intriguing as no one thing works, or lifts up every human being. However, some people got so charged to succeed through these seminars that they lined up to make payments after the function was over. It was quite a feat in marketing, presentation and delivery.

My train of thoughts took me back to my early days in India. Growing up in India, I recall people depending on gods and goddesses, or seeking blessings all the time of ascetics—*SADHUS, SANYASIS* and elders. Unfortunately, **the science of harnessing the life force is 'lost' in India**. The masses in India keep beating its shell. In the entire presentation, the felicitator did not mention the word, God, or name of any person! It is all within you, was the focal point.

Thus on this one day, in the morning, I was the center of a circle; but in the evening, I was one of the many points on its circumference. Both the school and PSI try to uplift people from their mire in life. One is free, and the other is not. One is a public school, not in profit making, and the other, being a private corporation, is for profit first. A school does not guarantee any thing when you finish it. The PSI returns $400, if not satisfied for any reason!

To emphasize this point, when the facilitator openly asked the audience if anyone wanted money back—not even a single person from my wife's group asked for it. Life and its secrets of success come in all kinds of packages. I am convinced that there is no one key that can open every door for every human being in this world. Search for one's key has to be relentless. **Self Realization is the other name of this search.**

(Feb 20, 2003)

WHAT IS YOUR PERFECT DAY?

I was asked this question a week ago—last Friday. It was an annual **Tall Tale Contest** organized by the Toastmasters. After the speakers finish delivering their tall tale stories, the judges go out of the room to tabulate the ballots. It is in this intervening period that the speakers are invited back to the podium for brief interviews, so that the audience may know a little more about them. Though a variety of questions were asked, but this was a common question. I was the third in line, when I went up. The perfect day is understood to be in normal routines over a month or two. It is not intended to be your dream day, or the best day of your life lived so far.

"My perfect day is to be able to read a book to its end—while sitting in a quiet library or in a bookstore—like Barnes and Noble," thus I put my answer. As compared with responses from previous speakers, the presiding female Toastmaster said, "That should be easy!" "Yes, in a way it is. I do start on reading a book, and quite often the book leaves me before I finish it," I added. She was a bit puzzled.

I clarified: For instance, if the contents of the book just do not hold my interest, I drop it. Or, after reading a few pages, I feel, as if I had read such a book by the same or other author, I stop reading it further. Most writers do have only one yarn, and they spin many books out of it. Sometimes, a thought enters my mind, as to, why did I not write on this subject? Or, I could write a better a book—then immediately, I quit on that book. I may return to the book for a second shot, at a later time, but for a while, the book has gone out of my hands.

I noticed that it drew some surprise looks from the audience. Then I added as story of a good friend and colleague (deceased now). of mine used to say, "Satish, read a book that is at least 100 years old. Time is wasted on others". Often it is true. However, I would tell him, "Abramowich, a book that is going to be 100 years old, has to be first one-day old, and then one-month old, and so on. So, how could I let them slip away from my reading pleasure without taking a chance on them as they are published?" He would just smile, and I noticed the audience smiling now!

(Mar 7, 2003/ May, 2011)

LIFE IS A DANCE, FOLLOW YOUR BEAT

There were two main reasons that I attended a recent dance program on the UNLV campus. One was that all the performers were at least 40 years in age, the oldest being 76. The other was to rekindle passion in my 11-year-old grandson who has been turned off from dancing for the last four years. It was quite an evening that it compelled me to look at dance as a window on life.

I am not a dance aficionado. However, I enjoy gyrating to my own beats. I grew up in time and place in Bathinda, where besides folk dances on celebratory occasions, dancing was looked down upon on a morality barometer. Amongst the upper echelon Hindus, girls would get some dancing lessons behind curtains and walls, but they were never permitted to display their talents in public. The attitude was applied to music, bands and singing groups.

There was no place for fine arts in the academic confines of schools and colleges. Now that I look back from the high plateau of the US life, mine was a totally different world. There were some socio-political reasons—like Islamic influence behind this stigmatic attitude against dances, particularly in northern states. Such taboos never existed in southern and eastern states of India, where Islamic influence was relatively weak.

Las Vegas is the ultimate dream of a showroom dancer in the world. Being a dancer in certain shows is no less than winning a Nobel Prize! Also, Las Vegas is turning into a haven for retired people. UNLV capitalizes on such a pool of senior expertise in getting them, as adjunct or part time faculty. Its Dance Department is one of the finest in the region, where students and instructors come from all over the country.

In all there were twenty-three dancers and twelve routines—including two Middle Eastern and three Spanish or Latin American. They captured different periods of the US life. Being staged in a studio, the atmosphere was intimate. At times, we were not more than 4-5 feet away from the dancers. Every dancer was at least 40, yet they belied and defied their ages during their performance! Their lower legs were fitter and shapelier than any 20-year old would have them. The skin was taut like the string of a bow that only fine creases were noticeable. Some had incredible sinewy physique. The 76-year-old dancer was just a marvel of flexibility and contours in her Tango routine! At the end of the show, I asked my grandson which number did he liked most, he named the Tango one. What a commonality between our generations!

My grandson used to go crazy while dancing on the melodies of his favorite singer Brittany Spears with his own electrifying fast moves and steps. A practice amongst the present generation of Hindus is to push their children in science and engineering. In his case, it became a family priority to steer him away from dancing—labeled as feminish. One day, he just dropped dancing. Later on, my daughter put him in soccer, swimming, baseball and tennis, but his heart has never found a home again. From a 6-year-old muscle ball, he has become so chubby that he drags his feet while walking. I was angry, but helpless against stereotype mindsets.

Too much of parental supervision is as harmful as too little interest in child's early growth. Having spent more than forty years in the field of education, I have come to a conclusion that there are infinitely many outlets for human creativity. The schools can channel kids into a dozen of avenues only.

While watching the program, my mind floated on to Hindu epics and mythology. One of the Hindu deities, is Lord Shiva, also known as *NATRAJ* (means king of the dancers). *NATRAJ* **symbolizes perpetual states of creation and dissolution of the universe as a cosmic dance**. It took me a long time to see a dance in mathematical symbols, say, in Einstein's famous mass-energy equation, e = m times c squared, and in the motion of subatomic particles. This idea is captured in the ***Tao of Physics,*** a popular book of the 1980s.

However, every motion is not a dance—like every brush stroke is not artistic, every note is not a melody, and every noise is not a signal. Nevertheless, I have seen dance in the gait of Balinese women. It takes place in the morning hours, when the Hindu Balinese women step out for their temples carrying flower offerings on their heads, or in their hands. It sets an ambiance, facial expression focused on divine, that lets the footsteps and swings of body parts take on to their rhythmic motions. The female curves and mounds make them ideal for dancing and for the arousal of man's sensual emotions.

Arjuna, the greatest warrior and archer of Hindu epic, the Mahabharata, was also a great exponent of dances. He taught dancing to the ladies of the palace during the last year of his exile term. That is exactly how I saw one of the four male dancers in the group. He must be in his 60s, but his body movements were telling the audience that they won't desert him at that stage! It was doubly inspiring to watch this mind over the body act. I am confident that one day my grandson will return to dancing with gusto.

May 13, 2003/Feb, 2012

POOR HEAT BEATEN UP IN USA

Today, I drove into the service foyer of Nissan dealership to have the brakes checked up. Getting out of the car and then going inside the service cubicle was hardly a five feet walk. A technician, while doing the paper work on the car said, "What a hot day it is!" We were in a centrally air-conditioned (A/C) environment and cars are A/C by the state laws. Any talk about weather is generally meant to fill some emptiness in a conversation. Being in an 'educator's' mood, I said, "Bill, talking about weather is like talking about poverty in Africa while living in the USA." He smiled at my pithy observation.

Today, the high temperature was 114 degree Fahrenheit that is more than 45 degree Centigrade. If it goes to 115 F tomorrow, then every weatherman has been telling that it would break a record of the hottest day set on July 12, 1979. They seek fun in it. Las Vegas is very hot in summer, but it hardy affects the pace of life. One comes out of one's A/C home, gets into an A/C car to work or shop in an A/C office, shop, or mall. Where and when would one feel any heat in the USA?

In Las Vegas, most public places are kept cold at 68 F (20 C) in summer that sedentary people have to wear light sweaters. My university office is so cold that every two hours, either I do 100 vertical jumps in the office, or simply walk out in 110 F to thaw my body! After the age of 60, blood circulation slows down and is cut off by the edge of a chair after an hour. Some of my colleagues in their 40s wear socks and light jackets in their offices to get the work done. I wear a sweater before taking a catnap in the office, as the body temperature drops by at least one degree during sleep.

This summer my classrooms are so cold that some students actually shiver and keep their hands folded in a math class! One justification is that cold temperatures control infections in crowded public places! Las Vegas casinos are colder. High rollers and casino executives prefer to wear suits and ties.

The TV channels and radio stations give weather and traffic conditions every 30 minutes. It serves a warning to the people who have really become 'softer' after nearly 50 years of life style of central A/C. Every summer, a tragedy takes place in Las Vegas, when a parent leaves a child or a family pet in the car to run an errand for a couple of minutes. In just five minutes, the outside temperature of 110 F turns the inside of a parked car into an oven at 170 F—enough to bake anything. In such a hot climate with humidity below 15%, there is no outward sign of perspiration, as it dries up, as soon as it oozes out of the pores.

The A/C has changed the landscape of Las Vegas. 100 years ago, there were hardly any white men besides a few thousand native Indians. Today, metropolitan Las Vegas, having more than 1.5 million people, is the fastest growing city in the US! Phoenix, Arizona, hotter than Las Vegas, has a population of nearly 2 million. It is all a conquest of heat by modern technology! Despite such a heavy power usage, Las Vegas does not face more than a couple of power outages even during summer months.

(July, 07, 2003/Apr, 2011)

JOB EQUALS TO GIRL

I have already told this story three times, so it is worth sharing it in print too. It happened a week ago, last Sunday. While working around midnight, Anupam's image flashed my mind. Since the downturn of high-tech industry, he has been professionally caught into a downward spiral. Even after accepting a huge cut of 60 % in salary, he could not retain his job. With wife and infant son, his frustration was rising, as the interviews, one after the other in Los Angeles (LA) area, were all unsuccessful.

As a last resort, he decided to accept a seemingly attractive 6-month offer in India. Having given a notice to vacate the apartment and sent family to his in-laws in Las Vegas (LV), he was busy winding up his affairs in LA. At the same time, half-heartedly, he had arranged two job interviews for the following Monday and Tuesday in Northern California.

I called up and told Anupam that going to India would put him technically backward based on my own experience. I have been out of the US three times from one to two years, and that is how I felt each time on returning here. However, I did not suffer financially. Then, I stressed upon him, **"Man in his 20s and 30s is driven equally by women and jobs. Not only that, he often measures one with the other!"**

Also, I reminded him, how six years ago, on first seeing Vinny for the first time in a LV wedding reception, he was completely bowled over by her stunning beauty and charm. During his three-day stay in LV, he not only won her heart, but also proposed her for marriage. Along the way, he convinced her parents, and his parents in India.

Yes, he did it all in three days, a record of some sorts in Indian family traditions! Nailing it on him I said, "If you like the job you are going to interview for, then you must take the same approach as you took for winning Vinny's heart. Sincerity, commitment and hunger must show in your eyes." "Yes," he responded briefly.

Two days later, on Tuesday night, Anupam called, "Uncle, I have news." I said, "I know, you got a job!" "Yes, it is a job that I wanted, and I am starting it tomorrow, on Wednesday", he added. A universal Girl-Job formula worked for him. Instead of moving to India next month, now they will move to Northern California—leaving Southern California, after ten years! **Beauty of life shines out in tougher times**.

(Sep 27, 2003/Feb, 2012)

COMMENTS

Mosaji, I don't agree that Anupam would have been technically at a disadvantage with his moving to India. In fact he would have been one of the management in that company, something which he may not grow into for some years here. In fact the offer was lesser than what he could have got in some other company, but was decent enough for a really good life style there. I feel that the issue is not as much the career as the sweat the heat and the dust of India. And an outdated public health and sanitation system. In fact all the "systems" in India could do with improvement. People are comfortable here, not necessarily mentally stable or happy. The constant insecurity takes care of that. It requires a very different person to be successful here than in India. Though a career in India prepares you for a lot more than stress at work. It prepares you mentally to be ready for anything and to improvise. An ideal country would probably have been people with Indian values with American habits, an American road, health, and other systems. We can dream can't we? **Aniruddha**

PERSONAL REMARKS

BELONGING TO THE SOIL

Eight years ago, I planted a pomegranate sapling in the backyard of our house. Despite no special care, it has turned into a huge bushy tree. Perhaps, this particular plant was just right for this soil. It yields a bounty crop every year that for its distribution, we run out of friends and relatives. A couple of days ago, while strolling in a contemplative mood in the backyard, I noticed that the north side of the house has shoots of another pomegranate reaching a height of 10-15 feet. **I did not plant this bush**. It is more than 20 feet away from the one that I did. A few years ago, I did notice some shoots were coming out underneath the cement slab that is only 18" from the block boundary wall.

I am very tolerant towards plants—including the so-called weeds that grow unattended all by themselves. I believe that they are truly made for the environment, if they are coming up without my effort. During the last couple of years, its growth has been very rapid. Some flying seed from the old plant must have germinated to a new root system. Being fully established, it is giving its first crop this year. Let me add that on the same patch on the east side, beside pomegranate, we also have an almond, plum and a fig tree. So far, none of their 'off springs' have been observed in our lot.

Suddenly, this train of thoughts turned inward in my own life. Thirty-five years ago, I alone came to the US. My younger brothers, sister and brothers-in-law just followed me wherever I was. They are now well established in their families and professions. This is common with plant behavior. However, when I went a step further to find a pattern in my coming to USA all the way from India, the analogy stops here. There is no flying seed that can cross fertilize even a couple of miles away.

Humans display a sense of adventure and control that is not yet observed in the plant world. Often I ask myself, am I a transplant from India?' To a certain extent, answer is still a yes, though I feel my transplantation is as complete, as the transplanted heart in a recipient 'feels' after a few years. There is no major rejection at any level. Humans also have a psychological interface and memory that tend to make a complete disconnection with any past a near impossibility. Yet, life is beautiful as it unfolds every day.

(Oct 15, 2003)

COMMENTS

1. Actually there are flying seeds which can transplant tens of miles from the parent. With the help of animal and birds (not humans) this transplantation can occur much further.

Now the eternal question "What am I" can be answered thousands of ways. Spirituality declares that we are all transients and in it transplantation has no meaning. Life as you said is indeed beautiful or Adhbhuth and contentment is in mind. **Rahul**

2. Hello Satish, It is good to hear that you are appreciating Life for what it is Warm regards. **Sarojini**

A WAY TO LIVE AND GO

No matter how much understanding one may have of Death, it hits inside when it strikes near you. It is like lighting that briefly appears as a beautiful dance of white bluish light in the sky, but it turns all into ashes where it strikes nearby grounds. Yesterday, on noticing Maureen, our neighbor walking alone, I asked, "Where is Frank?" "He died," she said it straight. Not believing what I heard and despite her matter-of-fact tone, for a moment, I thought she was joking. Getting closer and inquiring again, she said that Frank died on December 15. It was more than two months ago, and no one around us knew of it! It does tell about connectedness of social life on a typical street in the US.

Frank and Maureen live in a house hardly 100 yards away from ours—on the same street. We have seen them around for nine years; a gregarious couple. Both used to walk 4-6 miles in the morning and 2-3 miles in the evening. They were often seen chatting with neighbors out on their front yards. Thus, they always seemed to know what was going on our street. Once seeing me working on my sister's car they stopped, and Frank fixed the problem. He knew about the cars, as he had retired as a technician from a Ford factory.

"On Dec 15, Frank woke up with body aches all over. He thought it was a winter flue, though we both had flu shots. At lunch, he asked for a bowl of soup and went to the bed," she said, "in the afternoon I found him half falling off the bed." At 7 PM, an ambulance rushed him to the hospital. He had suffered a massive heart attack and was Gone before midnight. A hospital volunteer brought her back to an emptier home.

For Maureen, it was the worst Christmas. Tears rolled down her eyes and I consoled her. Thanking me, she continued on her Lonely walk—a stark reality of life. They were married for 44 years and had no children. She fondly reminisced the two years before marriage when Frank served in the US Army.

This is not the first time that I learnt of a neighbor's death after a lapse of a few weeks. You just don't see people beehiving a home, like in India, on hearing an illness, as it all shifts to a hospital. Frank made a connection with my *Reflection* on **Walking** that I personally gave them a hard copy on

Dec 11—four days before his death. They found it very interesting. Frank was frank at 75.

At age 10, one never knows of death; at 20, one is immortal; and at 40, death is distant. At 75, begin to enjoy life, as if having Bonus years!

(Feb 20, 2004)

COMMENTS

I remember this couple—very sad to hear Frank is gone, but Maureen is still walking. For a time, if we are lucky, we'll find a companion to walk us through life. But often one finds themselves alone on a path—the way we are meant to be. Marriage is a very unnatural state of being, but like many things we adjust to it. However, when two people separate-either naturally or unnaturally-the resilience with which we bounce back to our solitary ways is amazing. Maureen, on her solitary walk, is proof. **Annie**

TIME TO KNOW WHAT YOU HAVE

I felt good throughout the day, today! For one hour, I sat on the carpet of my study and resolved to organize papers and folders piled up on a section of the floor. A couple of times, while doing a through job of vacuuming, the pile was temporarily displaced and reset afterwards. I cleaned away five folders containing papers and documents; 2-3 years old. I did not have a stomach to apply a psychological principle: **If you don't remember what a folder contains, then simply trash the whole thing**. At my stage, forgetfulness means selective recalling—as only so much of the present and past can occupy the top of the head. Future is relatively short, yet it does occupy some space too.

My sorting means looking 'fondly' at every piece of paper. Some I touch for the last time before tossing them in a trash can placed next to me. Quite a few go into my writing clipboard, where the blank sides are recycled as work sheets. A few that still survived were filed afresh. I have four three-ring folders of my writings, but have a small two-shelf bookcase. In order to stand the folders, some books have to be taken out. First to be pulled out were three books on Ayurveda (means science of life) that a friend had sent from India. Immediately, I put them in a manila envelope and mailed them to my daughter-in-law, who is finishing her fellowship in nephrology next week. She has shown an inclination to learn about Ayurveda as well.

Then came out five big books, publications on Indian culture by famous Gita Press, Gorakhpur. They were shifted to a bigger shelf in the living room. But in order to make room there, I had to remove the first authorized English translation of the Quran in two large volumes. Now a Domino Effect has set in. The question was: where do I take the Quran?

I called the Dean of UNLV's world famous Lied Library about donating them. She was gratefully delighted to accept them. I personally carried them along with two other books; one on Vedic Geometry and the other on Vedic Astronomy. After 20 years, I said good-bye to them! I am sure a lot more people shall find these books useful for years to come.

There is a time to collect, time to treasure, and time to savor and enjoy any collection. Whenever, you feel overwhelmed by them in any manners, then it is time to give them away. The rule applies to decoration pieces, sundry items, knowledge and money. The pleasure is many folds when you are able to distribute them yourself. At a deeper level, it applies to life itself—letting it go when the Time calls up!

(Sept 02, 2004/Feb, 2012)

COMMENTS

1. Uncle, Neelesh here. I like the last 2 lines of your article. Very interesting!!! Best Regards, **Neelesh Garg**.

2. The world is pushing and pulling me to accumulate to an astonishing amount. Why? So silly of me to keep so much "stuff." There's my mate with the same malady. We found each other and our house is bursting out of bounds. Anjali, come and help me. Your writings are interesting. Especially the shorter ones. The long, long ones are very difficult for me at this time. Meaning that I'm too impatient. Hugs**, Dutchie**

3. For me also sorting out papers and putting them in orderly files/folders is a big problem. I sort out some and forget as to what extent I have done it. Forgetfulness is increasing day by day along with inner body strength and mental alertness. I ALWAYS TELL MY FRIENDS AND NEIGHBOURS THAT 'YOU ARE NOT ALONE'. THANKS FOR E-MAIL. **NIGAM**

NEW STARS ARE BORN

One's success in a field is also measured by the number of persons inspired to follow in a similar direction. Today, I felt a degree of validation in my new domain of an 'unpublished' writer. There is a growing mailing list of over 100 friends and relatives, who receive my aperiodic ***Reflections***. It was nearly two years ago, when I started sharing my observations and experiences of life. In this process, I have benefited a lot, though the decision of 'going public' hanged on my mind for more than 10 years.

Soon after I started writing, Vicky, son of close friends in Malaysia, wrote me a couple of times of his innate desire to write as well. I encouraged him in more than one way. **Writing is unraveling one's inner recesses before the readers.** It is no different than taking a shower in men's common area, or posing nude for art students.

After a year of dilly-dallying, Vicky wrote his first piece three months ago. Subsequently, the second piece came out. When the two pieces in succession came during this weekend, I knew he was on a trajectory to discover his new identity. Vicky is 30 and came to the US six years ago. His style jumps out of a blend of his tranquil life lived in South India with the high-speed US life of Silicon Valley. He drives BMW, works and resides in Sunnyvale with his newlywed wife 'imported' from India. There is freshness in his ideas that a writer's success is guaranteed.

The other is Anand Bhatia, recently retired business professor—living in a small town Victorville, California. We got to know each from our contributions in an Indian weekly—20 years ago. His style is smooth and conversational. Having a poetic bent of mind, his writing mixes poetry and prose. Out of a dozen, he has shared only three stories written during this year. Themes spin around his extended families in India and the US.

In communication, reading and writing are counterparts of natural modes of listening and speaking. We all love to speak up. Writing in prose, poetry, short stories, plays, letters etc are the cultivated forms of speech. Initially, it takes an effort, but with mutual support of fellow travelers in this caravan, the progress accelerates. A bottom line is: Don't suppress your mine of experiences, particularly, if you are nearing 60. It is no different from some people in India, who a few decades ago, used to pile up all their life savings in a pale and bury underneath in a secured ground. They did not know that the secret of wealth lies in its investment in public projects.

Congratulations, Vicky and Bhatia for setting your own blaze in the firmament! Welcome to a fraternity.

Oct 10, 2004/Mar. 2012

COMMENTS

Thanks for the words—u have made me popular. **Vicky**

Dear Bhatnagar Sahib: Thanks for writing about me in your latest "reflections" . . . . I am in the habit of writing daily and have been doing that since I was 15 years old. It is just that I do not necessarily send my writings to everybody. Again, to quote a poem in Hindi, *"Duniya me rehta hoon, misale taro-tambura, jara chede se milta hoon, milale jiske gee chahey"*. Moreover, "Words are like leaves, and where they most abound, much fruit of sense beneath, is rarely found!" Thanks for your kind thoughts, anyway. Affectionately, **Anand Bhatia**

My dear Bhaisaheb; All this while, I have been following quietly the various shades of your writing. I have enjoyed reading them and sometimes reflecting on a few of them silently. To me they come as expressions of a sensitive mind reacting to the everyday experiences of life in a guarded manner. They appear as true reflections of a keen observant mind. The writer in you deals with the themes carefully, sidetracking the sensitive emotional aspects of the story treating it as if from a distance, leaving the emotional involvement of the writer in the background. A blend of a journalistic approach with a storyteller's style to writing on sensitive themes. All the pieces are close to life, and you show a rare relish which is getting reflected in your writings. **D. N. Bhatnagar**

WHAT IS THERE TO LAUGH AT?

"I know there is nothing laughable", reacted my wife, when I told her of my 40-minute hearty phone conversation with Behls yesterday. She has also known Behls for 33 years, as I have. We share with Behls memories of our early days in USA—struggles to get settled. More importantly, we belong to the same culture of Punjab; its rustic honesty, loud laughters and robust work ethics.

A month ago, I gave a speech in my toastmasters club for a humorous speech contest. Essentially, I humorously conveyed that without the laugh machines used in every TV comedy show, people just won't laugh. If you have ever seen the taping of a TV show, then the audience is constantly cued to laugh and applaud. I hardly find any TV comedy show genuinely funny. They are so much piped and canned!

I told my wife, "Making some one laugh is not easy. I am not that young to burst with laughter at clowns, antics, or crazy gestures. If I am noticed laughing, then the comedic situation deserves high marks!" The demand for comedy shows is directly proportional to the fast pace of life. It is a challenge to make people laugh, as they are burnt out at jobs, isolated, or too absorbed in work.

When was the last time you saw two persons laughing in an office hallways? People will either declare you crazy, or disruptive. You are supposed to laugh only in front of a TV or in the privacy of your room. Actually, people only mimic laughs—prompted and conditioned by laugh machines. Comedy is a billion dollar industry. No wonder, Jerry Seinfeld gets paid $5 million a night at the Caesars Palace Hotel and Casino in Las Vegas!

There is something deeper when it comes to enjoying jokes, music and food. No matter how long you have lived away from your roots, certain jokes, favorite tunes and childhood dishes never leave you. They seem to cut permanent grooves into the psyche. All of us have favorite tunes from our teen years. I hum mine subconsciously all the time. Likewise, a deep fried *PRANTHA* with a butter stick placed on it, though no longer advisable for health reasons, but once in a month or two, when I eat one, it fills out every pore of my body! Jokes amongst close friends are no different. They never go stale, because they also capture a landscape of life gone by. So, laughing and eating with close friends, without any inhibition, qualms and reasons, is investing in a long-term happiness!

(Oct 24, 2004)

COMMENTS

1. Hello Satish; Talking about laughter, a friend of mine in Kuala Lumpur orgainsed a Laughter Conference which was held at the University of Malaya a couple of years ago and we invited a speaker from India, one Kataria, who had inaugurated many laughter clubs in India, to be the main speaker . . . . there were both theory and practice sessions. My friend also started a laughter group which was initially well attended but fizzled out when she left for Australia to further her studies in holistic therapies . . . all projects need enthusiastic leaders I think who can infect others with their own enthusiasm. Warm regards. **Sarojini**

2. "Laughter is the best medicine" so goes the old saying. In my morning walk from 5 to 7 at the local district park, there are laugh parties. It is said that laughing is useful for both physical and psychological health; it removes tension and is good for heart and brain. However, most of the members of the laughing club do it artificially. Real laughter is seldom seen or experienced, although every one claims to have it . . . . However, I feel 'something is better than nothing' and even the most artificial laugh is to be accepted to tone us up physically, mentally and psychologically. **Nigam**

EVERY DAY MIRACLE

One's knowledge and deeper beliefs are tested during an exam and a crisis. Our five-week-old grandson, Taj alias Anex has been feverish since last Saturday. Yesterday, a nurse, on the phone, suggested a medicine. In the evening, till 10 PM, we held him and he looked fine. But our daughter, Annie's motherly instinct did not see him normal. Today, in the morning, on noticing Taj's temperature running 100 degree, he was taken to his pediatrician. By that time, the temperature had shot up to 104. The physician rushed Taj to a hospital emergency in an ambulance with oxygen mask on his tiny face.

Around 1 PM, my wife called me in the office. Taj's deteriorated condition requires ICU stay for three days. As this news sank in, my mind went on fire! My first reaction was, "Some bad intention has befallen upon him (*KISI KI BURI NAZAR LAG GAI HAI*)." My mother of six sons, being highly protective of us, used to talk about black magic. I grew up ridiculing it, but gradually began accepting it as a lost pseudo science. Its variations are in every old society—particularly in China, Africa and South America.

As I composed myself, host of other reasons ran up. Annie and Taj have been around everybody just after two weeks of his birth. A period of 40-day seclusion for the nursing mother and infant has been a common practice in many cultures. It takes that much time for the baby to build some immunity against the virus and bacteria of the new world.

Taj was born three week prematurely. But he looked a weakling for only one week. Until this setback, he had a glowing aura about him. That drew an evil eye! He has been the center of attraction at three family gatherings. Last week, he was taken out to an office in a 110-degree temperature. No matter how comfortable the car temperature is, an infant cannot adjust to a 40-degree differential. My whole mind was racing to identify a reason.

Taj is lucky that medical diagnosis, coordination of health providers and best timely treatment were started within 15 minutes. An infant is like a flower; either in full bloom when well, or limpid when unwell. I brought my mental energies into focus on Taj for pulling him out of the red zone.

Annie, though tough, cracked on seeing her son reduced to a lump. Fortunately, a large number of family members, from both sides, provide a solid emotion cushion. At 10 PM, Taj was out of the woods, but Annie and Alex are keeping a vigil all night. The diagnosis turned out to be an infection that shot up to the brain. The source of this bacterium is still unknown. His tiny hands, legs and chest are all hooked up with tubes for I.V. and antibiotics etc. I consider that a miracle in action. The US indeed is a land of miracles—not of black magic, but of great scientific discoveries and achievements.

(Aug 01, 2005/Mar, 2012)

COMMENTS

Hello, As many of you know last week Taj was rushed to the hospital in intensive care when his temperature rose to 104 degrees. After a series of agonizing tests, he was diagnosed with bacterial meningitis and his condition was very serious. Luckily the doctors were able to treat him early enough, so there has been no effect on his brain, but it took several days before the fever finally broke. The good news is that he is doing much better. He is still on antibiotics and will remain in the hospital for 21 days to continue treatment to make sure there is no relapse, but the doctors all seem confident that he will recover well.

Despite the fact that he has gone through such a difficult time, Taj has already proven himself to be a strong little fighter. It's a wonder how he still manages to look so adorable even with IV tubes and wires attached all over him!

We want to thank all our family members and friends who have shown their support for us throughout this horrific experience. Alex and I truly believe that your thoughts and prayers are helping Taj get better. We can't wait to bring him home! Regards, **Annie**

JOY OF RE-ACQUAINTANCE

The sources of happiness are very personal. Two months ago, while talking with a friend of 40 years, Ranbir's name cropped up. Ranbir Singh Sidhu was the best student in my very first year of teaching in Government Rajindra College, Bathinda (BTI) during 1961-62. No one forgets the first experience in any walk of life. Ranbir went on to do PhD in math. We briefly met in Kurukshetra in 1967 and then in 1987, in Amritsar. The era of the 1950s and small town environment I grew up in BTI meant that once you know some person you never forget, as the names remain in circulation amongst common friends.

A month ago, I got a call from a person visiting USA. He said, "I am Jaidev Gupta—did MA in math in 1960 from Panjab University, Chandigarh." He got my phone number from my wife's second cousin who has been known to Jaidev for many years. Being senior to me by one year, he remembered little about me. It is the juniors who often know their seniors! That was the prevalent academic culture.

Today, I called Phani Deka in India. Hey, it requires a gut to call a person like this. We both joined Indiana University in August 1968. He studied geography and I mathematics, but we lived in the same room-for-rent house, known as the India House in Bloomington. For a few years after his leaving IU, we communicated, but lost touch in the shuffles of life. It was two months ago in Davis, CA, while talking with my son's friends couple from Assam, I remarked, "The Assamese are the most sincere people I have known in life." I mentioned Phani Deka's name. Lo and behold, the young woman said, "If Phani Deka went back to Gauhati—a city of 500,000, then he and my father are close friends!"

When you talk with a person after a gap of 30-40 years, it doesn't obviate the gulf of time. The excitement, joy of making connection and re-living some old memories are like seeing old photo albums. During 3-4 decades, people change enormously and in that process the mutual memories fade and shade differently.

Ranbir remains a quiet and reserved person. Though my student, but he just turned 65, as I am. In India, retirement means losing a zest for living. I get a thrill in calling and that is all is to focus. Jaidev retired as a high profiled bureaucrat after joining the elite Indian Administrative Services. In a position of power and influence, one gains in business type ties, but eventually loses sincere friends and relatives. Deka quit teaching, did MBA, and retired as banking executive. We all have raised children and now live in empty nests.

However, the minds are rarely empty, and it constantly explores new networks. Fortunately, my *Reflections* provide a new medium of discovering each other again. We can't keep on talking of a few rusty pieces of memories. You cannot milk anything beyond a certain limit. This joy is like finding lost money in the pages of an old book that was read years ago. It may not have much monetary value in today's economy, but it brings a smile, nevertheless.

(Aug 08, 2005/Mar, 2012)

UNIQUENESS OF A GIFT

It is a common practice to take out presents for the hosts, particularly, when one has to be a houseguest. In India of the 1950s, a box of sweets was the most welcome hand-carry gift. In the US, as home cooking is becoming extinct, a popular trend is to take the hosts out for a dinner. As regards buying a gift, during the last four months, personally, I have been in a shopping mall for hardly 30 minutes!

For the last few days, I was tussling for finding a memorable gift for a close friend and relative. When the mind subconsciously stays on a question, then an answer emerges in a mysterious manner. The gift that struck me is a collection of letters that the father of the host had written me during 1980-1995! He died in 1996. Its uniqueness lies in the rarity of long associations between persons, and the preservation of their correspondence at one end. That is why some letters of the famous are auctioned every year for tidy bids.

It is a mark of no less than a genius presenter to match a present with a presentee, and occasion. A few are good at it. **By giving a present, you can insult a person on one extreme, or enhance his/her prestige at the other end—and of course, anything is conveyed in between**. There is a whole history of gifts and presents amongst the rich and famous in every culture. A degree of thoughtfulness is necessary in picking a souvenir. For instance, a year ago, we had to tell a close relative to stop bringing gifts for us.

This collection has sixteen letters, beautifully written in a long hand. Though they were written to me, but they contain a lot of family tidbits and history. In 25 years, the unborns have grown into adults, and children have their own children, etc. I read all the letters for the last time in a couple of hours, as if bidding them good-bye. It had taken another two hours to search and pull them out from my massive files and boxes of letters.

The smallest unit of history of a nation begins from the history of a family. In a fast moving society, the family has come under blows. In that respect, my letters may be a small step towards a giant goal of **Know Thy History**. The letters reveal man's perspectives on life, as a grandfather, father, friend, husband, uncle, scholar, and so on. More importantly, they shed light on many practices and trends of that era. The letters are written in several formats that alone are interesting to notice. It is a Smithsonian experience on a mini scale! For example, the cost of a US aerogramme went up from 22 cents to 45 cents during this period, and so on.

Above all, it is a strange personal catharsis. A sense of trivialization of past events of significance enveloped me. Some incidents were forgotten! This is an incredible experience. It does not mean that one should not fight and strive for new goals in advance age. For me, one lesson is that a tree is as important, as the forest, where it grows.

(Sep. 24, 2005/Apr, 2011)

COMMENTS

1. Are you also collecting e-mails from your friends? Your gift of letters is indeed unique. I can imagine your boxes and files. It is known to me that if you wish to get rid of a friend, start spending on him. That is why you had to stop a close relative from bringing gifts. **Subhash**

PERSONAL COMMENTS

2 + 1 IS NOT EQUAL TO 3

In some instances, the pace of life in India has outstripped the US one. Yesterday, I spoke with two young men during a two-hour span. My 33-year-old nephew, in Chandigarh (India), works almost seven days a week for 12 hours a day! Yet, he is very happy for his salary and fringe benefits. The paradox is that he has no time to spend the money he earns! Three years ago, when he joined the company his pay checks lay undeposited for months, since he had no time to go to a bank and open an account!

What a contrast in job conditions in India from what was prevalent only a generation ago! His biggest concern is, "Uncle, the boss wants me to keep the cell phone turned-on all the time. Many a times he calls me, while I am driving on the narrow, windy, hilly roads. I have escaped accidents, but the boss does not care. His life is busier than mine." Obviously, India has a long way to go before it becomes litigious.

The other young man is a 30-year old, single and working in Atlanta for GE multinational. Having come from India eight years ago, he is very happy with his first job after finishing a US college degree. He owns a house and visits India every year. He has no belly fire for marriage, but works from 7 to 7. Neither he feels the need to socialize, nor does his Hindu religion mandate any weekly or monthly obligation.

This is becoming a very common phenomenon. A good financial package can take a person away from anything—be that family, temple, social life, sports etc. It is equally seen amongst professional women in India and the US. **Life is reduced to living only in one dimension of one's profession**. Last year, I was in Banglore and the quality of life that my IIT nephew and his wife (married in love) were living just shocked me. They have no time to look into each other's eyes. There is no space in life for a child, if married before joining a profession, or no space for a spouse, if single in a profession.

It does not matter whether one is married or not, the carnal desires are constantly satisfied in bits and pieces round the clock by magazines, movies, videos, TV and billboards. The distinction between pornography and non-pornography material is all gone! The front covers of all magazines at the US grocery counters are splashed with beauties wearing string bikinis and bras. Inside there are pictures of a few young, and handsome studs, seldom seen in real life. The rage of hormones is sublimated by profession, or vicariously satisfied with media. On cable TV channels, one can live in any sexual fantasy and perversion in the privacy of one's bedroom. The two-dimensional life on screen and print has taken over the three-dimensional real life.

It is in stark contrast to the holistic three-dimensional life my generation lived only 40 years ago! There was free time to do things during job hours, and time to read, write and relax with friends, colleagues and neighbors at home, and on the streets.

(Oct 09, 2005/Mar, 2012)

COMMENTS

Dear Professor Bhatnagar, What you describe the '2+1 ≠ 3' life in India is actually a part of 'India is changing fast' in various ways. My two sons in Delhi who are both in senior managerial capacity in MNC's are actually having 24 working hours. Their mobiles are always on not only to instruct those whom they supervise but also to receive feedback from them all the time. Sometimes, one of them who is in GE in Gurgaon returns only at around 3-4 am.

My son Ajay who is here with the US Oracle Corporation is planning to spend the Thanksgiving Week with family touring around some places in the Western part of the country including possibly Las Vegas. With best regards, **BSY**.

FACETS OF DEVELOPMENT

At present, the development of a city or nation is measured by a spate of construction activities. This has often bewildered me. A pertinent question is: Can a community develop without a rash of buildings mushrooming up? It depends upon a focus. In a capital-oriented economy, construction is synonymous with development.

Associated with construction projects in India are the unconstructed thatched hutments of the labor force. They are seen from groups of 2-3 huts to 2-3 thousand of them in metropolitan cities. Actually, this number is directly proportional to the size of a construction project. This aspect of urban life always strikes me during India visits. In contrast with the US, at my UNLV campus, a million square foot building is under construction, but not a single unskilled labor is seen on the site or living near it.

In Delhi, Bathinda and Chandigarh the prices of land and commercial properties are comparable to the top real estate prices in the world including Hon Kong and New York. Incidentally, my US hometown, Las Vegas is the fastest growing city in the country!

Today, I went out for a walk around 11 AM. Building a house in India is like baking a cake from scratch with all ingredients. Concrete mixing, plumbing and woodwork are all done on the construction site. The houses in Sector 21 of Panchkula area, where I stay, are priced in a range of US $100,000-300,000. With diminishing number of children in the family, particularly, amongst the Hindus, on the average, 2.5 persons live in a home.

A naked contrast in social strata is seen in an adjoining empty plot where an improvised tent is pitched and a laborer family of 6-7 lives in it! The night temperature drops to 40 degree F, but the entire family essentially sleeps due to each other's body heat. There is a sheet of rags to cover the bare floor and a blanket of rags on the top. At daytime, one sees only a frame of 8-10 sticks bent in arches and poles. A will to live defies its conditions.

It is a glaring scenario of human existence at extreme ends. I saw a 2-year old infant sitting in middle of a street and a car slowly driven by him. The mother was sitting with another infant in her lap working on daily wages—not too far away. A 14-wheeler truck drives by inches away from the kids, who claim the streets as their playground!

The ties of labor and industry are ancient. The laborers of brick makers are known to live near the kilns, but far from the city limits. They move with new kiln sites. The labor forces of industrialists like Birlas and Modis are known to be 'bonded' and work for them from one generation to the other! There is no kindness to a slave until he/she is free in spirits. **At the same time, the progress of mankind depends on mining—whether it is of minerals, electronic data or human potential**. In India alone, the palatial buildings and hutments are seen to exist side by side—like the two sides of a coin.

(Dec 21, 2005/India)

COMMENTS

Development is also measured by the QUALITY OF LIFE AND CULTURE; but it is truly measured by concern for others, which is an attitude and which does not mean sharing one's wealth. **Subhash Sood**

A BITE OF ENLIGHTENMENT

What is common between a place of worship and a hospital? The answer is not difficult. One goes to a religious place to seek inner solace and reaffirmation of beliefs enshrined in the mind. However, people go to hospitals to get well from physical ailments and injuries. The temples cater to the soul and hospitals to the gross body.

Last Sunday, two successive events took place. In the morning my wife and I escorted Anand Yogi, an itinerant Hindu preacher, to the Hindu Temple. His morning discourse to the congregation was set up there. I told her that afterwards, she and Anand Yogi would get back home with my brother-in-law, as I was to visit a former colleague in a hospital.

Anand Yogi's discourse focused on the transient and evanescence nature of sensory pleasures. He talked of the infinite love of God for human beings to be mined by dedicating lives to Him. He assured the congregation that eventually this love will permeate to make life blissful. At the end, when he invited questions from the audience, he was urged to continue speaking for a few more minutes.

After the sermon, I straight away drove to a hospital. All the time I was thinking how I was going to see Michael in his eyes. I did not even call him about my coming to the hospital. Michael's physical conditions defy description. Two weeks ago, both legs were marked for amputation, but the right leg is temporarily saved by a new procedure. The diabetes is slowly eating his body away. One eye is gone, and the other has little vision. He is on dialysis twice a week. A few years ago, he had a multiple cardiac surgery.

Despite these debilitating health problems, Michael has been thriving in mathematical researches! Though he took retirement for medical reasons 15 years ago, he continues to engage faculty members in his research problems. Thus, Michael has helped them in their promotion and tenure. When I entered the room, he was on the phone discussing a math problem. After 15 minutes, he engaged me into other problems.

It was amazing to watch this man not complaining or seeking empathy for his plethora of problems. He is both reconciled and not reconciled with the deterioration of his body in bits and pieces. However, his spirit has transcended his body! Michael told me that without these health problems he would not have done a large body of math researches! I was aghast, as who in sane mind would invite health problems to do intensive research?

Suddenly, I felt enlightened! It was in a hospital room; not in a temple, mosque, church, or gurdwara! Buddha was enlightened under a *BODHI* tree, but nobody else got it from that tree. Newton was enlightened after observing an apple fall from a tree. Since then zillions of people have seen apples fall. **Enlightenment has no special place and time, it just strikes into the receptive and inquisitive minds.** If nothing is permanent in the universe, then why not to accept it as God's plan, I posed it to Anand Yogi, one day.

(Feb 15, 2006)

COMMENTS

May be the enlightenment would not have come if you had not been to the temple and Anand Yogi's *pravachan* before visiting the hospital. **Ved Sharma**

Inspiration, oddly enough, comes when we have a problem with life (physical ailment, mental ailment, losing your job, losing a loved one). Michael feels he now has a finite amount of time left and bless him that he chose to do what he loves to do with more conviction. I don't see this as an inspiration of spirit or God, simply the man who had six months to live and chose to make the most of his life. It does sound extraordinary that a person has such spirit, but that is because all we are doing is comparing them to ourselves (who have health on our sides). I am sure that you too would be an inspiration in your last few months of ability (as long as you know ahead of time that you only have a few months).

I don't mean to downplay Michael's spirit as I am very impressed when people are inspired as opposed to falling apart because they think life is unfair. My point is that the inspiration was always there and it is ironic that it is realized only when we know death

I don't believe enlightenment comes from a place or an idealogy; it comes from within and very rarely before the glimpse of death. I feel that people are too self absorbed to see the greater good in themselves unless forced to and when they finally do I don't feel surprised, I feel sad that it took so long. And trying to figure out where it came from (Church, Hospital or Tree) is futile . . . it always comes from within no matter the religion or belief.

In a way you are helping me with my point.

For me the idea is to live. I am not worried about immortality or God, just what I can feel, see and hear now. I find peace in what is (Tarak), not what hopefully might be (idea of Tarak). Thanks for the reply. **Tarak**

I wrote: You are almost nailing the root of the metaphysical universe. Unless an experience is a gross or subtle extension of our sensory experiences, it is not acceptable to me either. Otherwise, God is not fair!! Stay on your right course.

3. Thanks for sharing this noble thing with me. I have additional ideas ALSO. I AGREE that BARRIERS are essential for progress and PROBLEM is the greatest STIMULUS. In that I think same as Michael does. **Subhash**

A THOUGHT TRAIL

Once in a while, I surprise an old acquaintance by a phone call. His/her surprise is my pleasure! Two days ago, I dialed a number in Chandigarh and spoke with a 'friend', Passi—acquainted since 1959. He was a year senior to me when I started my master's. After a year, he moved away. Though we have never met each other more than 3-4 times since then, but we sporadically knew about each other's professional directions through common friends. In India of 1950s, ours was a close-knit world. **Emotional closeness in a society is inversely proportional to its speed in communication.**

Hardly a minute into conversation that Passi obliquely asked, "Is there any specific reason for this call?" Perhaps he was more surprised, when I said none. We talked about a few friends and my *Reflections* that he has been receiving since last January. After the conversation was over, my mind stayed on his subdued reaction. In today's fast-paced life styles, unless there is a reason, we don't call anyone; don't knock the neighbors' doors, or even visit brothers/sisters. Social spontaneity is vanishing from daily routines.

My random callings to lost and found people reminded me of a lady whose life was profiled in the *Reader's Digest* more than 25 years ago. She lived in Midwest. Every year, during the spring season, she used to buy large quantities of flower seeds. During her drives, she would stop and spread a handful of seeds on the roadsides. It went on for years. Gradually, some seeds sprouted, flowers bloomed and their seeds, falling on the ground, germinated next season into new flower plants and bushes. After a few years, everyone started noticing the beauty of flowers on both sides of the roads.

Thoughts—like bullets, ricochet in incredible directions. I went back into what Passi might be thinking. He had a few seconds to wonder, as his wife had picked up the phone first. As soon as I identified myself, she called for him. A couple of hours later, I thought of calling him again and seek his help in establishing an annual prize in the name of Professor Hans Raj Gupta (1904-1988). I learnt from Gupta how to think mathematically, and how to teach. His influence remains the largest in my professional life.

This prize is to be given to the best student of MA Part I. The reason being, Gupta taught only a paper (a US two-semester sequence) required in MA Part I. Generally, prizes and medals are for the top student of combined MA

Part I and II. In India, it is very difficult to establish an ongoing award and I thought that Passi may help it out.

Isn't it amazing how thoughts bounce from one point to the other? In computer science binary logic has transcended into **fuzzy logic** 30 years ago. The next leap is into **quantum computing**. No matter what, the simulation of human brain and its circuitry of neurons and their firings will remain the common goal of computer scientists and microbiologists in the foreseeable future.

(March 06, 2006)

COMMENTS

1. After reading today's reflection, I was prompted to ask the question as human beings why is it so difficult to interacting with others. My first thought was people just don't have time to sit and talk whether it is with a spouse, colleague or just a friend. The desire to make conversation is based on "I need to know" and if someone approaches you without this sentiment neurons start firing in all directions and one becomes very defensive.

As I sit in my fish bowl office; let me explain I have office in an inner square and I am able to look out of the window and see 50 offices with 50 people on multiple levels and yet I know nothing about any of these people. All I see are human machines, clicking on plastic tabs, processing data, passing on information and exchanging ideas. What I don't see is facial expressions, dialog, laughter, anger and excitement. Have we become so robotic that the neurons that fire off in our heads are translated into electrons that move from PC to PC? When I examine this thought further, I realize that human interaction is nothing more then applied physics moving at the speed of thought.

Why have we reduced ourselves to find conversation through this academic discipline, why to do find laughter only through images on a plastic screen, and emotions expressed through electronic means? What ever happen to voicing your opinion on a street corner, meeting a friend to have a lively discussion or reaching out to someone in a social setting and saying "your ideas are inspiring"? Bring back those days when people can see, feel and experience conversation. I still look forward to your first publication. **Madhu**

2. Life is meant for SURVIVAL. The outcome of SURVIVAL is PLEASURE. Communication is one way of SURVIVAL. The outcome of a healthy communication is PLEASURE. PEOPLE HAVE FORGOTTEN THE VALUE OF COMMUNICATION. It would be a nice idea to offer a perpetual prize for Mathematics. Thought producer is not brain cell. **Subhash**

A FACE OF HOPE AND JOY

Taj, our ten-month old grandson, spends a good deal of daytime with us. That brings fresh smiles in our mundane routines. There is no way to ascertain it by any *Reciprocity Principle* that he also feels it to the same degree! When we had our children in this age group, I was too much wrapped up in my career building pursuits and other adventures that their infancy did not impact enough my mind. It was due to the joint family system or three generations living together in which our two older kids grew up in Patiala, India.

Yesterday, while watching Taj's moods, my mind jumped to certain principles of human development. The foremost says: **be fearless**. Infant is born with fear; fearlessness in cultivated to some extent. It is fun to watch Taj's fear and sense of insecurity, as if he already understands the adult world around him. It seems an infant sees some kind of demons even at daytime, when suddenly it starts crying. Or, an infant may be seeing angels, when a few-month old infant smiles without any control while eating and drinking.

Have you ever watched an infant holding a thing in its hand? He really brings the force of an adult, when you try to pry open the fist. Sharing is absolutely a cultivated trait. Further an infant's security consciousness through sense of touch is very strong. For instance, my wife cannot get away from Taj even for a second. He wants absolute attention.

The adults adore babies. Last Friday, in a restaurant, while the food order was waited on, I picked up Taj and walked over to the restaurant bar to check the game scores. While I was watching the scores on the TV, some patrons seemed to have switched from their game to Taj, who was giving them smiles left and right.

A baby is a symbol of hope for the parents, society and nation. Life does not live off any one glorious spot be that in the life of an individual or nation.

(May 07, 2006/March, 2012)

IT IS ALL ABOUT GROOMING

Yesterday, a friend told me of a dialog between two 7-years old girls; that he had overheard in a fitness club. One girl bragged of having a boy friend, and added some salsa by telling that she had kissed him. The other girl inquisitively looked at her and asked, "Have you kissed him all over?" My Indian friend was dumbfounded.

Kissing and hugging are in the fabric of the present American culture. Since infancy, the kids get sneak previews of sexual adventures by catching their parents or 'significant others' in beds/sofas, watching porn movies or finding adult magazines in bathrooms and bedrooms. The world of internet has brought pornography only a few clicks away. By and large, the kids are exposed to active sex by the age of 5-6 at homes, streets, and in the schools in the name of sex education. Putting contraceptive on a cucumber is a part of public school curriculum today. President Bill Clinton lowered the morality bar when he repeatedly told the worldwide TV audience that oral sex was not an intercourse. Since then oral sex has become safely popular, particularly with preteens.

Fifty years ago when I lived in Bathinda, I still remember a 6-year old boy, living with parents and siblings in a thatched hut, talking about sexual intercourses. It had shocked me as a college student. The sexual promiscuity amongst the gypsies (**GADIA LOHAR** of Rajasthan) has been proverbial. Desire for sex is independent of time and geography.

In the US today, local news quickly become global. Recently, Gloria James made sports headlines for driving under the influence. It is no big deal in USA, as drinking and driving are unavoidable in independent life styles. Senator Edward Kennedy has been guilty of it. In Gloria's case, the juicy part is that she is the mother of LaBrone James, 21-year old NBA player, whose contract at age 18 (6', 8"; 240 Lbs.) was over 100 million dollars! He was born when Gloria was 16! One can interpolate her sexual flings, while growing up in the ghettos of Akron, Ohio.

My thought on Gloria was that, all things equal, the probability of healthy kids being born are far greater to 16-year old girls than to 36-year women. It is the quality of seed that makes a difference—whether in plants, animals, or humans. With childlessness and infertility on the rise in the US, mothers—

like Gloria, should be rewarded! Incidentally, LaBrone James' father was a convict, and so was Gloria's second boyfriend.

Being into the tennis season, the son of tennis legends, Andre Agassi and Steffi Graff, has been exposed to tennis since birth. It is also OK for the kids showing promise in music and math. But the society is not made of a few areas. I was not alarmed at this conversation between two 6-year old girls. Should it be encouraged or not, is to be left to the parents. In the US today, beautiful little girls are groomed to be models, showgirls, and call girls (if mothers are). In 1975, when our daughter told that her 10-year old friend was wearing 60-dollar dresses, it needed no guessing what the mother was grooming for.

(June 07, 2006)

COMMENTS

Reading your articles on sex, I get feeling that you are passive aggressive about this issue. It seems that part of you wants to talk about it openly and a part of you wants to condemn sex. There seems to be a lot of confusion in your writing. Also what is Morality? I like to know about your views? Oral sex is bad. Pre-marital sex for man is good but bad for woman. **Rahul**

PERSONAL REMARKS

A DAY'S WORKS

"How was your day?" yesterday, I asked a cardiac surgeon acquainted for many years. "I performed two open heart surgeries today", matter-of-factly, he replied. "That means the surgery time of 10-12 hours, during its pioneering stages, is now cut down to 3-4 hours", I remarked. Yes, he said. The conversation changed to different topics, as we were amongst 200+ guests at a wedding reception.

With my favorite drink of Gin and OJ in hand and mingling with friends, I ran into another surgeon. I often tease him that with deep baritone voice, he can have another career in the US. Heart surgeries still on front, (subconsciously, I may need one), I asked, "Tell me the most exciting surgery that you have performed." Oh, was he ready! "A 21-year old girl was brought in a hospital for C-section delivery. During the labor pain, suddenly all her vital signs including heart collapsed. A helicopter ambulance brought her to the hospital, where I was on duty, and heart surgery facilities were available. On opening her up, I discovered that rheumatic fever that she contracted as a child while raised in El Salvador, had infected a major heart valve. The C-section bleeding had complicated the problem. The surgery took seven hours. The surgery was successful, yet the girl did not regain consciousness.

"Neurosurgeons declared her vegetable, but I suggested a re-habilitation plan. Two months later, I went to check her in the hospital. Right then, she opened her eyes and asked, "Where is my baby?" That was a year ago. Last week, she along with her husband and baby came to thank me!" I was in awe like the others who were listening to this story.

Well, as if to fully satisfy my curiosity, he told me the case of a 70-year old. All his blood was drained out and body temperature brought down to 18 degree for a surgery to be completed within 45 minutes! Odds were 100% death without surgery, and not much less with surgery! He said the man was enjoying his breakfast this morning! The first case has been published in a reputed journal of vascular surgery. This makes him more proud of his surgical expertise.

Several thoughts swirled my mind. No matter how routine surgeries may have become, in a litigious US society, he has to do his very best each time. He mentioned, "The moment I saw the girl I told my self that I won't let her die; so young and beautiful." Just then, his wife, a beauty of her own, walked up to him.

In my subject of math that I love to teach, it boils down to touching the lives of the students through instruction. It is a challenge that I try to live up to every day. My classroom is a 'surgical' theater. For my surgeon friends, saving and extending lives is a daily routine. In ultimate analysis, they are touching human lives. Yes, staying at the top of one's profession has to be a cardinal principle. Incidentally, both are ranked as the top cardiac surgeons in Las Vegas. I know people who wait to go under their knives!

(Sep 03, 2006)

COMMENTS

Dear Satish, Your surgeon friend must be flying high! Solving problems in such a grand way lets his heart sing and head burst with enthusiasm and joy! Your story of your pals is an inspiration (as always) and arouses many strong feelings in me. One feeling is the feeling of elation when I solve a problem. It's beyond words to tell of the euphoria that pervades my mind when a solution is discovered. It's almost a manic reaction. Hugs, **Dutchie**

I have the experience going under the Knife; it might have taken four hours. I left the hospital a day after the surgery. I thank God for all His mercies. I kept on top of my field till I retired. I still keep up on all the advancement that is of great interest to me. You take care. **Matt**

It is a great story. The surgeon did a great job. But the lady woke up weeks after the surgery, by divine plan. We control the effort, not the results. **Cyriac**

ON ASSEMBLING AND DIS-ASSEMBLING

Was I happy today at my achievement of assembling a revolving leather chair? Last Sunday, when I walked in with two big cartons—one containing parts of a pedestal lamp and the other of a chair, my wife naggingly declared, "You won't be able to put them together." She is right. For the last several years, I have lost interest in garage activities. But just for this very reason and give myself a boost, I bought them!

Putting the lamp together was nothing, but I was stuck half way with the chair. My wife kept talking of the dangers of walking into the room with parts strewn around. I too was in quandary and thought of calling my brother-in-law, who can fix anything. Yesterday, on noticing the chair in my office being of the same kind, I figured it out. The only right sequence is to screw up the right arm with the seat, screw it up with the back, then the left arm, and finally back again. I declared mission accomplished!

For having an item assembled in the store, one would pay @ $50/hour. For the stores, there is a lot more to it. The breakage of the household furniture will be phenomenal, if assembled furniture items are shipped across country. Also, the floor space in the store that had 20 boxes in one pile may not be enough for more than 2-3 assembled ones. There is a public safely factor too.

Assembly line for super mass production was perfected by the Germans and brought to the US after the WW II. The amazing theory behind is that any complex job when divided into the smallest units, can be finished by unthinking persons. A thinking person on an assembly line will be fired at the end of the first day!

The concept of assembling applies far beyond putting the furniture items together. At UNLV, three ongoing construction projects are: a huge 6-storey parking garage, a 5-storey science engineering building, and an Olympic size recreational complex. It appears that the architectural specifications go to the factories. Various construction items—from the ducts, pipes and rods to 4-6 ton beams come on time to the sites precisely marked. It is awe inspiring to see 200'-high monster cranes lifting hefty beams and girders, and gently placing them where two men at either end align them in place. On weekends, the iron workers weld and rivet the steel frames. The work force at a construction site has dispersed into planning offices, factory productions, coordination, transportation, and scheduling. The number of people employed is perhaps more, but they don't make shanty colonies near construction sites, as seen in the big cities of India.

The invisible aspect of industry is packing and shipping. There is a lot of mathematics behind packing and transportation theories. In 1975, a mathematician won a car filled with men's toiletries for guessing the answer closest to the exact one! It turned out to be a simple math problem for him. Today, my assembly project filled me with the same delight, as I notice in my grandson finishing his Lego structures. For adults, it is therapeutic too, and the fun is at the end. **In ultimate analysis, life is all about a cycle of assembling and dis-assembling!**

(Sep 13, 2006)

COMMENTS

1. In my opinion life is about challenges, accomplishments and love. **Dutchie**

2. Satish, I beg to differ with you on the subject of assembly lines. Henry Ford the First was using assembly lines long before WW II. A kind of assembly line existed in England as early as 1801 by a company that made something for the Royal Navy (see "assembly line" in Wikipedia). Other points on the subject of constructing the steel skeletons of buildings: 1) The joints are either welded or riveted. Solder is pretty weak. 2) A friend of mine back in Dearborn, Michigan (the probable birthplace of assembly lines in the Rouge plant of the Ford Motor Company) worked for Ford and had something to do with building construction both in Canada and the US. He observed that in Canada there were many workers scurrying around during the framework construction. In the US there were few workers and they mostly appeared to be standing around. However, the steel skeleton got built a whole lot faster in the US. You are certainly correct about the design of packages. I have a friend who was in the business, I think. He might even be induced to talk to one of your classes. **Dave Emerson**

FALLING IN THE FALL

In a way, the US is a funny place. Nearly forty years ago, when I came from India to USA, it used to surprise me—on hearing about the beginning/end of the football season—likewise, basketball, baseball, hockey etc. In Punjab, where I grew up, the word 'season' meant only weather—like summer, rainy, winter, or spring, though the Webster does define 'season' in a wider sense. Also, the US has hunting seasons—deer, fish, rabbits, ducks etc. The hunting games are governed by *logistic differential equation* in math!

The fall season, also called autumn, symbolizes the falling of the leaves from the trees. Its beauty lies in the colors of the leaves, when they are about to fall. The tourists visit the national parks in Midwest and northeast to enjoy the riot of various hues—bright yellow, pink and red. It appears, as if one is walking on a psychedelic carpet and listening to a soft music created by the crackling of leaves under the shoes.

In Las Vegas, one has to drive 150 miles north at 6000' elevation to watch this natural extravaganza. Most of north India, being at a lower latitude and elevation, doesn't have this natural *HOLI,* an Indian festival of colors! There, the leaves change colors while attached with the branches. Once they fall off, they turn into crusty brown within a day.

I often wonder—how come this stunning beauty of the leaves before their 'death' (detachment from the trees) is absent in human beings at the time of their death? I have raked my brain in identifying one 'common' sign of beauty in dying persons—be that at physical, mental, or spiritual level. There has to be one. That is a quest my life!

Having spent a good deal of life on the campuses of US universities, I love the fall (first) semester. Fall semester/quarter is a 'spring' time of newly admitted students. UNLV student body is unique in the country, as one can notice students of any age group—from 17 to 70. They are all young at heart, and curious to learn new subjects.

Walking around the campus is like strolling in a park with colorful leaves all around. Every day, there are campus activities—like enticing and inviting new students to join a club. The off campus organizations—like various branches of the US defense forces, religions, banks are permitted to set up their booths. It is fun to watch them pitching.

I encouraged my freshmen granddaughter, studying in UC San Diego, to join or start, Hindu Students Association—like the ones UNLV has of the students, who are Muslims, Jews, Mormons, and Christians. The banks and financial institutions give out little things—like T-shirts for signing up for their credit cards! It is a modern robbery and open sharking the naive youth, but it is legal. Gone are the days of the students getting weekly or monthly allowances from their parents. Now the parents are at the credit mercy of their own kids!

(Oct 12, 2006)

COMMENTS

Satish, The color of the fall foliage in the Midwest is pale by comparison with that of New England. I lived in Michigan for 21 years (including graduate school) and the best foliage years were barely the equal of the poorest years in New England. I was born in and grew up in Massachusetts, lived a year in Connecticut, and lived a year in Vermont and three years in New Hampshire while doing my undergraduate work. One who knows, **Dave Emerson**

Title should have been FALLING IN THE FALL. Well you have written a wonderful article, very enjoyable. **Subhash**

A DOMINO EFFECT ON CACTUS

Life never fails to amaze me in its most trivial existence. I have seen persons, plants and pets half functioning because of paralysis of one side. In India, through the 1980s, the 'stroke' was often confused with 'heart attack', though both health problems are as old as man on earth. I have seen trees half-green and half-dead. According to the horticulturists, all the ash trees on UNLV campus have some disease. A few times, I have seen trees in the forests vertically split off; half burnt out by a lightning bolt, but the other half standing. However, it is the first time that I have seen literally half of my 10' high cactus felled down.

The 'pedigree' of this cactus goes back to at least 20 years. I clipped a leaf from our previous house and planted it in the smaller section of the front yard soon after we moved into the new house 12 years ago. It really took off. This particular fruitless cactus is a very stubborn that it absolutely defies any pruning for shaping up. It may be compared with most non-conformist persons, who are creative at extreme ends.

For general safety of the visitors and there being limited yard space, I regularly clip the nodes heading in 'wrong' directions. The new nodes are removed as soon as they 'burst' out of the peripherals of the leaves. While shaving them clean, I always think that there has to be a recipe to pickle these buds or sauté them. My gut feelings are that they have tremendous medicinal values. But so far, I have been gutless about ingesting them!

Last week, for three days, the gusty winds in the valley had bended a 'string' of cactus leaves. Mind it, each cactus leaf weighs at least 2 lbs. They are very solid, though they get all the nourishment from the air through millions of needles and thistles on their surface. There is little nourishment from rocky ground—besides, it has small root system.

In December, a friend came over to visit, and he was astonished at the sight of this cactus in height and 'symmetry'. Last Sunday, when the wind had eased up, I stopped to examine the possible damage. I clipped a leaf to save the others and was pleased that it had survived the howling winds. **Perhaps, the half was waiting for me to say good-bye**! The very next morning when I came out, the devastation was terrible. For a moment, I thought someone had vandalized it out of jealousy! The winds had already weakened one-half and now broke it off from the bifurcation point of the second node 'level'.

A 'string' of 2-3 leaves, each weighing 4-10 lbs, makes an unstable formation. Imagine an half 'tree' containing 4-5 such strings falling in a domino effect, thus, ripping away many other leaves on its way down to the ground. Consequently, other ground cacti were crushed for no fault. But a cactus seldom dies!

My thought switched to the high rise towers (50+ storeys) mushrooming the skyline of Las Vegas. It is reported that the steel frames of the towers can withstand an earthquake of 8.0 on Richter scale. But the internal and external elements of nature weaken the structure in sections. It is possible that an earthquake may damage only one-half of a vertical structure, as the winds have done to my cactus. One life form simulates the other!

(Jan 17, 2007)

NUTS AND FUDGE OF LIFE

"The fudge that held all of nuts together" was an inscription on a marker in a neighborhood memorial park that was noted while strolling there. It was written about a man who had died at the age of 68. Planting trees and laying down engraved stones in open spaces are also the ways of writing a local history. It is a part of the head stones that are commonly seen in graveyards, cemeteries and memorial parks of the funeral homes. Memorial signs are also seen around local community centers. It secures a piece of immortality as long as someone knowing the deceased is alive or a stranger, like me, finds it interesting.

Ten years ago, my children, nephews and nieces pooled $150 to have a pine tree planted and a stone reset in a nearby Sunset Park. They did it in the memory of their grandparents who had left very fond memories for each one of their grandchildren now in their 30s. This park project, based upon emotions, generates money for public amenities. A plant and the stone do not cost more than $20, but the amenities the money provides in the park and recreation are incredible by Indian standards. The public restroom, (toilet) that I happened to use yesterday was absolutely clean. The stainless steel toilet bowl was shining, toilet paper roll was in place, soap for hand wash was in the dispenser, and electric hand dryer was functional.

In every aspect of public life in the US, private funds are raised to keep the standards high—whether of research in a university or facilities in a small park. If the public officials think for public good, then the good ideas are easily braced by the public.

While I was amused to read the wording, soon I began to muse over it. Mind is very amazing in reacting with sudden encounters and connecting them with whatever is on its front burners. From the marker, I visualized that the words captured the gratitude of the sons and daughters of the deceased. They may have had diverse personalities and traits to pull each other apart, but this man, perhaps, kept them together as long as he lived.

My thinking was in a natural order of my experiences, since all seven of us—consisting of six brothers and one sister, have divergent personalities. The negative sides of diversity are blunted and toned down, as long at least one parent is alive. Parents make a family glue. Again, it is not all positive about the glue either. However, un-gluing is an evolutionary phenomenon, as the siblings get married, raise their children, and move away in their professions. When my father died, I, the oldest, was 31, and the youngest one was 14, who looked up to me as a father figure.

Our mother died ten years ago. Her relative long presence was positive overall, though the ties were not always warm between every two of them. Now, there being no parent left, the nuts are surely getting nuttier! However, life goes on with or without fudge, but there are moments of gratitude for the fudge that I also felt in the park yesterday.

(Jan 26, 2007)

COMMENTS

Relatives must cause trouble if you are not unhappy. Life is there to be loved. It is ancient Hindu wisdom that we are ONE. **Subhash**

FLIGHT TIME HANG-OUT

Every day, America takes consumerism to new heights. It struck me during a recent flight. Consumerism combines with psychology, researches, surveys, and statistical analyses in a dynamic fashion. People are constantly moving and changing their attitudes and habits. Every airline has a monthly flight magazine and seasonal shopping catalog. It essentially means that you can remove your shopping itch even while flying five miles above the ground. That adds to the excitement. It is like making love in the sky that I once read in a novel many years ago!

During flights, browsing through the flight magazines could be worthwhile pastime, rather than time killing. I seldom complain about the flight stress except occasional swelling of the ankles caused by being stuck into a seat for more than two hours. Actually, I forget to stand out of the seats and aisles to kick away blood circulation. My in-flight activities are reading, writing, munching and drinking. Flight magazines have short readable articles. For instance, this week, I enjoyed reading an article on the US cell phone usage in foreign countries.

A 15x15 crossword puzzle took the best part of my flight time—solid two hours! The crossword puzzles enhance the ability to retrieve right words that I constantly need it in my writings. Of course, I did not finish it with all my efforts alone. Some puzzle clues are still beyond me—though I have lived in the US for nearly 40 years. They are cultural in terms of music, life styles and other peculiarities. I used the keys in those items. Yet, it was quite a mental exercise to get the rest right. I don't recall the last time a crossword puzzle absorbed me for so long.

Men act differently when held captive under any circumstances. My wife always complains about her journey—whether driving or flying. For her, the two end points alone of a journey are important. I enjoy all the infinitely many points between these two. The truism, *'Life is a Journey, Enjoy the Ride'*, the corporate logo of Nissan Autos, speaks after my heart.

The usage of the word 'Never' should never be left unbounded from above. I deliberately broke this pattern of not looking at the catalogs. For the first time, I amused myself with every page of the shopping catalog. Never before were seen so many pictures of the watches in one place. They were dressy, pricy, heirloom, under water (for fish finding), and hiking (with GPS) watches. Also were the shoes with springs and non-adult massagers for body points not easily reached.

Two hundred pages of the catalog contained over 2000 items; mostly exotic—like, golf ball finder and latest products of the Sharper Image. I went through every page with a vengeance. Next time, I may order something. It was a discovery of a new fun in doing that I always avoided before! Sales catalogs, coupons and flyers coming in the mail everyday are trashed right away! However, during this flight, it was informational and educational. Consumerism, when looked as circulation of money and development of variety of skills, is creative and never wasteful!

(June 01, 2007)

A PENNY WISE

I don't hesitate to pick up a 'lost' penny lying on a curb or roadside. Before putting it in a pocket, I play a little guessing game with its mint year. Usually, I am off by a year or two. It is exciting when I am absolutely right, as it makes me feel more intuitive on that day. It is, perhaps, a good exercise to enhance one's intuitive power.

Why do I pick up these 'drop-out' pennies? It is money, though not a whole lot. I don't buy the argument that one drop of water at a time will fill a bucket. What good is that water, if it takes a lifetime! In my subconscious mind, the pennies, on the ground, remind me of scarcity and poverty that I have lived and still see in India. Money is not meant to be thrown away.

Picking pennies is like picking deserted pets on the streets. Many organizations work for retrieving pets and providing them shelters. Who cares for the pennies? Is there a cultural reason for not picking them up? I have not explored it. But so far, I never had any bad or good luck with them over the years. I did hear about not picking a penny once it falls out of hands or pocket. Actually, curbside change often drops out of a pocket, when stepping out of a car.

How do I end up finding them? Well, I love walking/watching my neighborhood at least twice a week. That is when invariably pennies spot out. Do I look for them? Not at all! In fact, I take my glasses off before walking, unless needed at a road crossing. Walking is having a dialogue with myself. So, I pick up the pennies that 'beg' me for a home, and directly shine out in my path.

For the last 10 years, I have been collecting pennies that are at least 25 years old. No specific efforts are put in this collection. Only the ones found during walks are sorted out. Eventually, every penny will be 25-year old, but that is not my thinking. How many 25-year old pennies do I have? About 70! They are not like stamps or other artifacts that the collectors periodically lay them out, and fondly touch and see them. All the pennies are in plastic film caps. Am I counting on any appreciation? I don't care. When I check out from the Planet, my kids may laugh at on finding them. However, it is joyous for being the only collector of its kind!

There is something typically US about this story. Nowhere else, I have found money in small change lying on the roadsides. There are two reasons—one, in other countries and cultures, people speedily pick them up. Since in the US, most people do not pick up the pennies, the poor penny wait for a person like me to come by, warmly look and turn them before sheltering them in a pocket. Yes, there is a piggy bank sitting at the kitchen counter. All the 'young' pennies are slided into the slot. My wife adds other coins now and then. In a year or two, when it is filled up, she exchanges them in a credit union.

There is something philosophic about penny picking? In a society, individuals are the smallest units. Sometimes, they are lost physically—say, during a hike, or mentally while working on a problem, or spiritually—seeking *Nirvana*. Once in a while, they may be helped (picked up) by a stranger, who puts them back on a track. There is a better place for every entity in the universe.

Jan 22, 2008

COMMENTS

Sweet story . . . . thanks . . . . It's the little things . . . . Ha ha ha ha ha . . . . yes, that's what I do . . . . just for exercise . . . pick up stuff . . . to bend and stretch . . . . keeps my back strong. **Dutchie**

You are right when you say that we pick up money because we do not think money should be thrown away, no matter how small the amount. I grew up learning the value of money so even today, if someone gives me money and asks me to spend any way I want, I will still be watching carefully and spending wisely. **Prafulla**

A REFLECTED STORY

The following story came in an email and promptly, I modified it for drawing a different lesson from a similar, but gentler experience:

"A man came out of his home to admire his new car. To his puzzlement, his three-year-old son was happily hammering dents into the shiny paint. The man ran to his son, knocked him away, and hammered the little boy's hands into a pulp as punishment. When the father calmed down, he rushed his son to the hospital.

"Although the doctor tried desperately to save the crushed bones, he finally had to amputate the fingers from both the boy's hands. When the boy woke up from the surgery & saw his bandaged stubs, he innocently said, "Daddy, I'm sorry about your truck." Then he asked, "but when are my fingers going to grow back?"

"The father went inside home and committed suicide. Think about the story the next time you see someone spill milk at a dinner table or hear a baby crying. Think first before you lose your patience with someone you love. Cars can be repaired. Broken bones & hurt feelings often can't. Too often, we fail to recognize the difference between the person and the performance. People make mistakes. We are allowed to make mistakes. But the actions we take while in a rage will haunt us forever. Pause and ponder. Think before you act. Be patient."

(A modified version)

"A man came out of his home to admire his new car that he had named as Maxie. To his puzzlement, his three-year-old son was happily hammering dents into the shiny paint. The man ran up to his son, and gently took him away in the garage. He picked up a handful of nails of different sizes and pieces of fire logs lying in corner.

"He showed him how to hold the nail with index finger and thumb firmly and then demonstrated how to strike a small hammer right at the center of nail's head. Then he walked back to nurse his Maxie. He promised her to take her right away to the best 'surgeon', the auto dent remover and painter.

"Hardly, had he finished consoling Maxie that he heard his son shrieking with pain. Slowly, he walked up to him and noticed his little index finger had turned blue with a blow of the hammer. It had slipped off from the nail's head onto his tiny finger. And he had guessed it so! That was his thoughtful plan of teaching him a life-long lesson.

"While rubbing ice pack on his tiny finger, he said, "The pain you are having is the same that Maxie is having when you were banging her with this hammer." To his amazement, his little son was not surprised! In the innocence of mind alone, one can grasp the unifying idea of the *Oneness in the Universe*. Some men achieve it after years in self-realization."

(Apr 04, 2008)

HIGH SPEED NOURISHMENT

"Drive it like a stolen car," said the service assistant while handing back the key of my car. I had gone there for having it checked up before undertaking 700-mile trip. This phrase amused me since it conveyed two meanings. The obvious one is that a car thief or hijacker drives a stolen car as fast as he can before the cops are alerted, and it gets faster when chased by the troopers.

The car had been giving a problem in its computerized engine configuration. A yellow sign, 'engine check' would appear on the screen. It would particularly concern my wife, who thought the engine was going to blow up soon. There are several reasons, as explained in the car manual. However, every time, it appeared, I would drive it to a nearby service center and have it re-set.

After 2-3 fix-ups, it was diagnosed that the problem was caused by the car parked idly for nearly four months, when I was gone overseas last fall. "Either leave the car for a day with us, or drive it for an hour on highways at high speed," was the advice. I took it upon myself, and on a weekday, drove it on Interstate—15. For a few seconds, the odometer needle kissed 120 MPH. Well, the diagnosis seemed right, as the sign has not shown up for two months.

It is a small 'sporty' Mercedes with, perhaps, 250 HP engine. In fact, the mileage/gallon noticeably increases after it is driven 300 miles on highways. The problem is that it does not happen more than once a year. I have lost some enthusiasm for driving and my wife's all gone. There is a well-established correlation between male sex and high speed driving. Life after 60, goes into different gears. It is reflected in slowdowns of physical reflexes and motions. Retrieval of facts from the memory bank is not quick—call it a selective memory or its overloaded shelves. After all, so much is unknowingly accumulated in home and brain as a by-product of a long life.

A nice feature about this Mercedes Service Center is that—like a personal physician, you have one service assistant for your car, as long as, he/she remains employed there. This guy knows the history of my car, though stored in his computer. Since this engine problem involved the US Mercedes, it got a little notoriety. By "Drive like a stolen car" he meant to advise me to give the car high speed blasts, so that this problem does not recur.

While musing on the benefits of high speed, it struck, that the physicians tell their out-of-shape patients that once a day, the heart must operate at 90% of its pumping capacity. Short sprints and calisthenics are essential for staying healthy. Getting out of breath is OK, as long as the breath is not lost! The sedentary life styles create all kinds of problems for human bodies; it is truer for automobiles too. Carbon deposits, in engine blocks, are only burnt away at high speeds.

However, there is a shift in mental speeds. It is a ***Principle of Conservation of Thought Speeds***. Lately, my mind has been capturing so many observations and connections for **Reflections**. But only 30 % are materialized! The rest, like the waves, go back to the ocean of thoughts. Did I have this speed of thoughts in my youth? Yes, but on different planes. Here lies a beauty and mystery of human life. I wish to unravel some high-speed secrets from other life forms!

(May 09, 2008)

COMMENTS

1. You probably have the secrets already buried in your own brain. All it takes is a little concentration to restore the ideas, memories, opinions and other types of thoughts. Hmm? Betcha I'm right. Hugs, **Dutchie**

IMAGE MAKES A DIFFERENCE

Last week, while browsing an Indian daily for the 'home' updates, it was pathetic to see A. K. Antony, India's Defence Minister being hand carried away by three army generals. Antony, age 67, had suffered a heart attack during graduation ceremonies at Khadagwasla, a premier Indian army academy. In his loose white clothes, either *Dhoti/Kurta*, or *Pajama/Kurta*, his unconscious body was lumpy. It was in sheer contrast to the generals in full regalia with stripes and medals.

The entire news coverage and picture were depressing. Defence Minister of India must always radiate the image and aura of physical and mental toughness. If the cadets and officers dress in the western uniforms, then the Defence Minister can go in a western or at least in an Indianized pantsuit. The *pajamas* and *dhotis* are simply out of place! They are OK in the Parliament. The Academy attracts media and cadets from foreign countries too.

The US election primaries bring out all the strengths and weaknesses of the candidates for its presidency. In Indian parliamentary system, a cabinet minister, being an elected member of the Parliament (MP), may not have any knowledge of the portfolio charged with. In a not-so-light vein, I was thinking of some 20-25% of the MPs who are under indictment for various crimes—including murders. If the MPs—like the late MP Phoolan Devi, were India's Defense Ministers, then Pakistan and China would have not attacked and occupied a million sq km of Indian territories. There was no way that the weakling Prime Minister (PM), Manmohan Singh would take such a decision. Historically, the territories of Australia and New Zealand were won from the natives by hardened British criminals, who can also be very patriotic.

The image is everything in any time and space. In the present video universe—a picture, splashed across the world, can create a tsunami effect. I remember the first visit of Indian PM, A. B. Vajpayee, to Srinagar, during ongoing Kashmir insurgency and Hindu ethnic cleansing. His wearing *dhoti,* in a public function, may have emboldened the Islamicists. The then Defence Minister, George Fernandez wore *chappals, kurta,* and *pajama* on his tall and lanky frame!

One wonders at the sense of nationalism of Indian PMs and Defence Ministers in public. The dress must fit the occasion and place. If the wardrobe is driven by some nationalistic consideration, then it is time to emulate the dresses of Hari Singh Nalwa, the general and Defense Minister of Maharaja Ranjit Singh. The military outfits of Maharana Pratap and Chatrapati Shivaji can be modified by India's famous dress designers. A sectarian leader in Punjab has been severely criticized for dressing himself like the 10th Sikh Guru, Gobind Singh. The masses universally admire the dresses of their heroes, and emulate them.

Antony was born, raised and grew out of the politics of Kerala, the state farthest from the political upheavals, which the northern states have suffered for centuries. Prior to becoming Defence Minister, he may not have thought on the dynamics of insurgencies in the east, west and north. After 60, you can never catch up on culture and history of every region. Moreover, a politician has his sights on the next election, seldom on the next generation.

June 03, 2008

COMMENTS

Bhai Shri Satish Ji, Saprem Namaste! You have a GREAT flair for writing, please keep it up. On dress Code : I 100% agree with you, the dress code MUST be a befitting dress to the occasion. **SC Gupta**

THANKS FOR CALLING!

"Who told you?!," comes like a sling shot, whenever you call a close friend, or relative to particularly check on health, greet on birthday, or a family news. Another social habit, irking me for a while, when during a conversation, again with close friends and relatives, the person at the other end suddenly says, "Please don't tell it to anybody else!" I don't utter a word in response—what to say or not. It has been happening with greater frequency that makes me wonder at the world I am living. Yes, a world, lived on 50 years ago, may still exist somewhere in cosmos!

Family manners are corollaries of the social culture around us. There is no specific length of cultural radius. We are the centers of our own circles. Last week, there was such an encounter when I heard on voice mail, a message from my brother-in-law in India. He, at 63, has come closer to me in 45+ years of our relationship. Hardly a month goes by when we don't hear each other's voice. Of course, he looks forward to my *Reflections.* From his recorded voice, I sensed that something was not right at home there.

It was evening; I asked my wife to call him back, while her B'Day was still 'going on', instead of waiting for him to call us again. His 38-year old son answered. With speakerphone on, the nephew was speaking tight with short sentences in concerning tone. Well, when I took over the receiver, the first thing I said, "Is everything OK with your Mummy or Papa?" He cracked up, and told of his mother's recent health problem. But at the outset, he said, "Please don't tell it to Bhua Ji!" I knew it was out of sheer habit of a conditioned mind. I did not say a word.

I was wondering that who else is closer to his parents than us. Luckily, his both sons are very caring and they are a happy joint family. Most seniors, of my generation, are not as fortunate despite, relatively speaking, being financially better off. That is not the point of this *Reflection.* The point is that why do we cloister in a cocoon about sharing our highs and lows of life. Years ago, I read that sharing multiplies the happiness and divides the sorrow (mathematically!).

Yes, I am trying to cultivate the habit of first thanking the person for calling me at points of my emotional extrema (borrowing a term from Calculus). An unanticipated call pleases me all the more. However, I don't discount people who are jealous of other's happiness and in hearts rejoice at other's miseries. But again, I am talking of my generation who are in their 60s. By this time, we have 'tested' all our near and dear ones. In fact, our circles are shrinking and the common Limit (again, from Calculus!) is not too far!

After a couple of days, I shared this news with my wife's younger brother living in the US. She snapped at me, "You should respect the privacy of others!" Respect for privacy is a new buzz phrase in the US—going to extreme. Back in India, there was no question of privacy when 7-9 family members lived in 2-3 rooms with windows and doors always open for the neighbors to see and hear anything 100 feet away. It is funny how people, particularly from the 'third world country' forget their moorings in the lap of luxury of the USA, or now newly found riches in India too. **Life is trying to relish all the experiences—sweet and sour!**

(Aug 09, 2008)

COMMENTS

Dear Satish, Yes, secrets are daggers in relationships. Openness and clear communications are essential in human relationships. Why keep secrets? And when asked not to tell a proposed idea or event my answer is no, don't tell me if you want me to keep it a secret.

If the request comes after the secret is revealed my answer is no.

Most of our peoples' and worlds' problems come from communication problems . . . either miscommunications or absent information. Hmmmm . . . . There's a mountain of philosophizing on this subject always. **Dutchie**

PERSONAL REMARKS

A MAN OF TOTAL PEACE

One of the popular stories from Buddha's life (called *Jatak Kathas*) is on total transformation brought in Angulmala (means wearer of necklace of fingers). He was a murderous dacoit who chopped a finger after the kill for a 'finger necklace' he wore to terrorize the masses. It was also known that within a radius of two miles of Buddha's camp, complete harmony prevailed.

Life is very strange. We revere great men and women lived in deep past, but often ignore the one living next door, though having comparable achievements. Like, one can never fathom the size of a mountain while climbing up on it. A distance gives a better perspective. Angulmala story cropped up in my mind when SN Subba Rao stopped over in Las Vegas for a couple of days.

I asked him about the psychological tools he used that lead to the surrender of over 600 dreaded criminals of Chambal ravines. **"Gandhi is my gun and devotional songs are my bullets**," thus lived Subba Rao, when he was amidst the bandits and their families. The world knows only the dramatic surrender of the first batch of gangsters before JP Narain on April 14, 1972. But that was only a beginning. It was the result of Subba Rae's incredible work—behind the scene that went on for 3-4 years. He was hardly 40 years old then! I asked, "How did you win their confidence; visit the places that police dreaded; deal with police and unprincipled politicians?"

Subba Rao is a man of few words with self-effacing personality. On the top, he practices humility of the highest order. Yet, I glimpsed a tip of the iceberg of his material on dacoits. A movie, bigger than *Gandhi*, can be produced on Subba Rao's life with Chambal dacoits, called the *Baghis*. He narrated the story of a dacoit who stayed with him—after serving 8-10 years in prison. During a school visit, a 10-year old boy asked, "How many men did you kill?" He gently countered the kid, "Can you tell the number of *rotis* you ate last year?" I was stunned at human limits in any direction. There are scores of such stories of legendary dacoits—like Surinder Singh and Mohar Singh. Madho Singh lived like a lamb in Gandhi Ashram Joura that I visited in 1980. A TV serial on many episodes will be a great hit. It is a call for the movie entrepreneurs.

For his monumental work of bringing peace in Chambal alone, Subba Rao deserves 2009 Nobel Peace Prize! No matter how one defines peace, it is always championed by one individual in one region. Thousands of civilians and men in uniform were saved from the jaws of death, and family tragedies averted due to this historic surrender. Subba Rao has demonstrated to the world that worst social problems have peaceful solutions too, provided a spiritual person of gets involved. Through his regular camps, he has been sowing the seeds of communal harmony and tolerance in the hearts and minds of generations of youth in India, and abroad for the last 40 years.

Greatness, in public or private life, is a result of perseverance for years. However, in public life, physical and moral courage are additional ingredients. Subba Rao personifies them. When I asked how he developed courage, he answered, "It came in a second when he once looked into the eyes of death." The nomination deadline is Feb 01. The website **nobelpeaceprize**.org has all the details. His peace work is greater than that of many past winners. Just *Google* SN Subba Rao.

(Aug 23, 2008)

COMMENTS

1. Impressive . . . . thanks. **Dutchie**

2. "Abu Ben Adhem (may his tribe increase) awoke one night from a deep dream of peace
   And saw, within the moonlight of his room Making it rich, and like a lily in bloom
   An angel writing in a book of gold. Exceeding peace had made Ben Adhem bold
   And to the presence in his room he said 'What writest thou?' The vision raised its head
   And with a look made of all sweet accord Answered: 'The names of those who love the Lord
   'And is mine one?' said Abu. 'Nay not so' Replied the Angel: Abu spoke more low
   But cheerily still and said 'I pray thee then Write me as one that loves his fellow-men'
   The angel wrote and vanished. The next night, It came again with a great awakening light
   And showed the names whom love of God had blessed. And lo! Ben Adhem's name led all the rest." The aforementioned is a poem I read in my school years. Here the name of Abu Ben Adhem's name can be safely changed to Subba Rao. **Rahul**

3. Respected Subba Rao Bhai ji is a Great courageous and thoughtful soul! It is difficult to find such living enlightened saints. He really deserves the honor of Nobel Prizeship. What a pleasant surprise that you have mentioned the historical occasion of "Bhagis surrender" which took place in Gwalior, when I met Dr Subba Rao ji for the first time and brought him home after the ceremony. God's ways are amazing as you know I met him thereafter in Fresno, California Hindu Temple from I brought him to our house, after over 36 years. There is a sea of change in us but he remains almost the same in zeal & spirit. He enjoys Divine grace! Kind regards, **Jadav (JR) Sundrani**

LANGUAGE DEFINES TRAITS

"hope u r doing well . . . I am sorry for not mailing u since long.
life in dese past 3 months have been quite a rush . . .
I got thru da entrance exam for Masters of commerce at delhi
university . . . classes
started within a week n i was waiting for my hostel list to come out . . .
now dat i am settled in da hostel . . . i catch hold of comp in da lab wenever i get time.
life here at da campus is cool . . . pacing up wid each passing day . . .
i am coming in da contact of various ppl frm diverse background . . . my
batchmates r fun ppl to be wid . . . i just hope i do wel . . . coming to home for 15
days in october for autumn break . . . wil send u regular replies den . . . .
dere r few reflections of urs dat i still need to go thru . . .
keep writing n take care . . . regards"

This is a recent e-mail in exact format that I just received in not-so-uncommon writing style getting popular in India. Most Indians (including movies) routinely mix **DESI** words (from Indian languages) with English in varying proportions. Generally, the text is in one or two cryptic sentences. I had to read this long one 2-3 times loudly to figure out the meanings.

Many things flashed my mind. I don't think that the French would ever excuse any one playing with their language. They take pride in its 'purity'. Hey, this e-mail is from a 21-year old niece. Gaining fluency even in this kind of writing is a sign of innovation! In college, I 'rebelled' in spelling certain words and grammar usages. It did not last long, as it cost me heavy in exams. However, it is re-incarnating since I started feeling my own boss in writing **Reflections**.

The British tried to Romanize the colonial languages. They succeeded in Indonesia, Malaysia, and Africa, but failed in India. They had limited success in Indian army. Phonetic slangs are counter parts of the written ones. During the 1970s, these slangs were a rage on the highway CB (Citizens' Band) radios amongst the truckers and new generation of 'cool' people.

But there is a danger too. It is like walking with a stoop; forward or sideways. Over a period of time, it becomes a cause of several health problems. The spine has to remain straight! Unless, improvisation is a hobby, one needs to be careful about any deviation from norm. **Normality is a virtue for status quo, but a bane for creativity.**

Youth is a time to experiment and explore the highs and lows of life. One can 'indulge' in some 'abuse' as there is time to re-correct it. This writing style may provide a new genre in poetry like the '4-letter words' have done in rap and metallic music. That has made a new generation of millionaires. But in a long haul, despite incredible flexibly in English language, there is a good English and bad English in the world of business, professionals, politicians, and intellectuals. During a hike, one must go off the trail for a while to smell wild flowers and catch sight of animals in the bushes, but getting lost in a forest could be fatal. Language usage is no exception!

(Sep 06, 2008)

COMMENTS

1. During a hike, one must go off the trail for a while to smell wild flowers and catch sight of animals in the bushes, but getting lost in a forest could be fatal. Language is no exception! Very well put. Regards. **RAJA**

2. "Hinglish" is an accepted thing in India nowadays . . . Let them "play" with the language. English is no more the monopoly of the British/ Americans. **Abraham**

3. Bad English is bad English! It is no excuse for creativity! Dr. A. R. **Bhatia**

MASSAGES AND THE GIRLS

Today, I had a full body massage done over by a young white girl! It went on for solid 55 minutes in a family massage center. It really transported me back to my days in Bathinda (BTI) of the 1950s. The girls were not seen in boys' schools, playgrounds, and bazaars. The college had hardly 20 girls; any interaction would invite disciplinary action. My story was peculiar as far as dealing with the girls was concerned. We were six brothers, and a sister was born when I was about to finish college. To add to this drought of girls, there was hardly any female cousin.

It was a dream to touch a girl consciously, and felt heavenly to be touched by one. I can recall so many instances when an accidental brushing of girls would electrify my entire body. Here I was, today, in my American brief, spread on a cushioned massage table under a thin sheet; half the time on the stomach, and half on the back. And a girl's hands were kneading over my body.

I told the girl about my doing regular oil massages. In BTI, Sunday massage with mustard oil was a public ritual. Now I massage while watching a sporting event on TV. It goes on for at least 90 minutes. This massage was essentially dry, as she used lavender with some liquid base that left no oily film. It helped her hands move easily while pushing the tissues and muscles along.

Though my wife is a frequent customer, but I have avoided it for a couple of reasons. Sanctity of my body not to be touched over by anyone is one, and waiting and driving time of at least two hours is the other. Today was an exception. Being a little coldish and feeling tightness in some muscles after yesterday's 10-mile walk, I decided to have them professionally loosened up.

Above all, I expected new material to reflect upon. In fact, I read my recent *Reflection* to the girl before entering into the dim hall partitioned by moving curtains. My wife was getting on the other side of the curtain. It was a family affair. The ratio of women customers over men was 3 to 1. Naturally, more female masseuses are employed than males. My wife told me that, earlier, they sought customer's preference, but now assignment of a customer and masseuse is random.

Certainly, I would have refused, if a male masseuse were signed up for me. Generally, the girl's hands being softer, it is more suitable for my skin turned sensitive by massages over the years and topped by meditations like *Vipashyanaa*. Since certain areas on the back cannot be reached, I instructed her to spend more time over there. Was I stimulated or titillated? Who won't be? The wildest fancies of men are all about women.

What an irony of life that I had to wait for nearly 70 years for such an experience. At the other extreme, it reminds me of an incident that took place in 1961. Three of us went see a movie in Kiran, the first cinema in Chandigarh. There was an incredible rush for the tickets. On spotting our female classmate, 'blacky' Kamla at the women's ticket counter, I suggested my friend to ask her to buy our tickets too. He barely touched her on the shoulder for drawing attention. She did buy our tickets. But the very next day, Kamla complained against us on the violation of her modesty. We were reprimanded for it! One could say, "You have come a long way Baby!"

(Oct 12, 2008)

COMMENTS

1. Better late than never! Best wishes. **Abraham**

2. Wonder if you could get the same massage as openly as now in USA 40-50 years ago. Times change as do values. **Rahul**

II.   SOCIO-POLITICAL SETTINGS (Interval)

POLITICS OF NATIONAL AWARDS

The *India Journal* of Feb 11 has reported that the sitar maestro, Vilayat Khan has refused to accept the Padam Vibhushan award of the Government of India. It is the second highest civilian award in India. In the past, he had declined to accept the 'lesser' ones, Padam Shri and Padam Bhushan, on similar grounds. He has decried politics in the process, particularly, when persons, not as talented as him, were recognized and awarded each time before him. Any public honor feeds the ego in gross or subtle way.

However, politics is an integral part of any award system. Take for instance, the Nobel Prizes in peace and literature, in particular. Some of the greatest giants in these fields have been denied these awards. In India most of these awards have been influenced by the Congress Party and persons closer to its ideology. It has continuously dominated the social and political life for nearly 40 years. Many great minds in various facets of public life, but having different political leanings, have been ignored for such awards.

It is the first time in the last 4-5 years that one notices the influence of the BJP Party and its supporters. They are trying to remove the inequity that has perpetuated for decades. With the result there is a lot more hue and cry over the awards than ever before. Over a long period of time, the human minds are gradually conditioned to accept any unfairness and wrongs.

Nevertheless, a few persons of the stature—like that of Vilayat Khan, stand up to restore luster and glory to these awards by not accepting them. I salute him for his courage of conviction. Padam Vibhushan will remain smaller, as long as, he walks by it with dignity.

(Feb 26, 2000)

THERE IS A TIME FOR SPORTS

On Sept 9, while watching men's semifinals of the US Open Tennis tournament, suddenly the cameras zoomed in to show former US President Clinton in his sports jacket and trousers walking in to watch tennis on a day, billed as Super Saturday of tennis. It is eight-hour coverage—including women's championship. He looked Healthy - waiving at the people around and shaking hands now and then. I wished to see an Indian PM or President engaged in sports in India.

Once President Clinton was settled in his booth, a former tennis great and current top color commentator, John McEnroe, was invited to join him. He spent 20-30 minutes with the President. During this time, the remaining two commentators of his broadcast team were jokingly wondering, as to what was going on between Clinton and McEnroe. Picture shots showed President Clinton alone doing the talking and McEnroe nodding his head most of the time. McEnroe has a reputation for a big mouth. Apart from his sharp insights into the game and players, he does not miss a beat in making wildest comments that often generate controversies.

Any way, McEnroe not uttering a word was actually timed for 4 minutes and one-half! When McEnroe returned to the commentator's booth, the play-by-play analyst, Dick Enberg asked him, as to what went on between him and the President? Promptly, McEnroe said it was between him and the President! However, in the course of subsequent commentary, he said the President has a keen interest in tennis and that is good for the sport.

It may be added that Clinton is the first sitting President to have come to watch the US Open. It struck me how he was aware of the historical importance of this event. He could as well be attending to zillion national and international issues always pressing for his attention. However, it does not mean he had completely disconnected himself from his work. McEnroe told his listeners about the health and senior citizen issues the President had on his mind. Getting away from presidential work to watch sporting events provide a space that is conducive for new ideas. It is a true Americana often witnessed!

My thoughts again went back to India, where sports are completely divorced from life, whether in academics or politics. During last summer months, I visited some ten schools and colleges in Punjab and Haryana. I did not notice even a single sporting activity in school grounds, nor any youth that could be identified from a competitive sport. Certainly, I met a lot of students who had excelled in academics, since my family has instituted academic awards.

I also happened to attend a session of the Parliament before my departure from India. Being a member of a Las Vegas Toastmasters Club, my objective was to see how parliamentary norms and etiquette were observed. I was disappointed for disregard to elementary rules of order. It all appeared a free shouting down, and not respecting the authority of the Speaker. The sports alone instill leadership and team concepts during the formative years of 10-20 years. Relatively speaking, Indian members of Parliament hardly appeared as specimen of a healthy life style.

I learnt first hand how entire India was riveted to every little thing that President Clinton did during his stay in India. Daily TV coverage continued for nearly eight hours. In contrast, it is shocking to notice that there has been no such coverage on PM Vajpayee's current visit to USA! As of Sept 13, I have not seen his name even once in local press or TV news. It is a reflection of what everyday Indian mass media covers that comes out of USA vs. what US media does to the life from India.

Another observation is that Americans make a clear distinction between an office and its occupant—say, Clinton, as a person and Clinton as President of the USA. No one ever undermines any office, and never of the US President. Clinton watched tennis for nearly four hours. He was always addressed as the President or President Clinton by every commentator. During my India visits, I often notice the office being downgraded with its occupant. **Institutions are far more important than any individual in any sphere**. Great nations are built only on the foundations of great institutions. Unless this intellectual and public awareness becomes a part of Indian psyche, Indians, whether in USA, Fiji, Guyana or in India, may be portrayed as very smart and successful individuals, but collectively shall continue to remain vulnerable and exploitable.

Sport is a paradigm of life in the US. Like in the US, sports can never be integrated with academics. Since India already has a few coaching institutions, it is high time to start separate sport schools—right from the elementary levels to high schools, where every conceivable sport and martial arts be the only new curricula apart from minimum doses of languages, social studies and sciences. The climate in India is right for the private enterprises to take a lead in this direction.

(Sep 13, 2000/May, 2011)

VATICAN AGAINST YOGA!

Yoga is a flagship of Indian heritage. It is India's best export, or gift to the world. By any estimate, yoga is a worldwide billion-dollar industry. The Hindus do not have monopoly on yoga anymore, since many foreigners have mastered its fundamentals. During the mid 1960s, yoga got some international notoriety when the Beatles gave a shady boost to the Transcendental Meditation (TM) of Maharishi Mahesh Yogi.

During the first phone conversation, Anand, a young itinerant yogi from India, claimed that his yoga techniques can make a person look 15 years younger. Having practiced yoga *aasans* (physical postures) since boyhood, I could sense his sales pitch. Anyway, I organized his eight yoga workshops on UNLV campus. Despite posting flyers at prominent places, only 4-5 white Americans came for it—though it was free. It puzzled me knowing that Americans do not go after the freebies. In Las Vegas, there are at least five yoga centers charging $10-15 per hour for instruction. Most companies hold regular yoga workshops for their employees. The yoga techniques and instructions are secular.

One day, on noticing a building custodian working around the area, I casually invited him to join Anand's workshop. He said, "**You can't recruit me!**" The tone of his response struck a strange cord in my mind. Nearly twenty years ago, the Vatican had issued an order against yoga. The Vatican believes that yoga leads one into Hinduism. This injunction against yoga bothered me for a long time. But this simple remark of the custodian suddenly unraveled its mystery.

For the nation builders, a fundamental question is what type of society is wanted. Look at the Hindus who have been doing yoga for over 2000 years. During the last 1000 years, the Hindus, despite making at least 80% of India's population, have been the weakest people in the world. The poverty of India of the last 100 years has taken her soul out. The present India is only a shell of its glorious past.

The yoga *aasans* are steps leading to such surreal concepts—like *MOKSHA* and *SAMADHI*. After all, what is the image of an individual doing yoga? It is of a person sitting in a lotus posture with eyes closed. What inner changes are wrought by such a practice? Certainly such persons are incapable of physical adventures on land, sea and space. They don't explore the frozen tundra of the poles, burning plains of the Sahara desert, or the dark bottoms of the seas. The yoga has not produce he-men for the WWF, players for the NFL, or NBA.

Above all, yoga does not inculcate any team spirit and togetherness. In ultimate analysis, its impact is generally otherworldly. From my personal experiences and observations of yoga practitioners, it is good for non-competitive and non-aggressive lifestyles. A misconception about meditation is that one gets enlightenment of all knowledge. Granting some knowledge, it can never be of modern science, arts and literature.

Therefore, the Vatican is not wrong in discouraging yoga, as its acceptance would lead to the acceptance of other aspects of Hindu life that are not at all enviable. In general, the values of Western lifestyle are very different from the present Hindu life.

Anand Yogi taught a total of twenty *aasans* for invigorating the body muscles, inner glands, and organs. Its sequence begins with all encompassing *aasan*, *Surya Namaskar* (salutation to the sun) followed by *aasans* for activating the brain cells. The last was an exercise of jumping on toes. He concluded each session with *Shava aasan* (dead body posture) for total relaxation. While he demonstrated, I translated his Hindi into English, whenever necessary. Despite wearing two unstitched sheets, he was able to do all the *aasans* with modesty and deftness.

Personally, my quest has been to rediscover yoga as a modern science of harnessing the mental powers through meditation. **Energy is then harvested and stored in the body that is readied through specific yoga *aasans*.** At the end of all, the energy is to be released and distributed for the welfare of the society at large.

Finally, yoga may help an individual to optimize his/her potential. But it is at the cost of the collective role in a family or society. **Historically, no two yogis are known to have pooled their energy in any one direction**. A vibrant society cannot let its men and women sit still for hours. I have no qualms with the Vatican's decree against the practice of Yoga. The key lies in moderation.

(Apr 06, 2003/Apr, 2011)

WHAT HAVE YOU BEEN COLLECTING?

Garage sale is an American institution. It took me a while to understand it. During early years of our arrival in USA, we could not afford to buy new items, and the used ones, we were reluctant to buy from garage sales. We were smitten by an Indian feeling that buying anyone's discards was undignified. Gradually, its acceptance started settling in our psyche. Now I find garage sales so interesting that I do not mind stopping or taking a detour for checking them out.

Yesterday, I was out walking in the morning that I started following signs of a garage sale. It was relatively a small family house cleaning that was perhaps set up for enjoying a good weather on the side. Often in garage sales, I look out for books, coffee mugs and baseball caps. The rest is secondary. Books, after a while, I pass them on to my relatives and friends. Mugs and baseball caps, I give them out during my overseas trips. They really make people happy, as I notice these items treasured during subsequent visits.

A book, on the top of a small pile was on *Philosophy of Leisure*. I asked the lady, "Have you read this book?" "No; actually the books are of my late father," she replied. The title really intrigued me that I turned the book cover and found it published in 1945. Underneath it were 4-5 more books on other aspects of leisure. They were not pictorial and travel kind of books. They were college textbooks. I just could not believe that 55 years ago, there was an academic interest in leisure as a subject.

Being a professor, I asked, "Was your father a professor?" "No, he was a policeman!" It really impressed me to realize the intellectual depth of a US policeman. She added that he loved to read and collect books. I said, "**If one has not collected any thing in life, then one has not fully lived it**." The woman responded, "That is exactly what my father used to say!"

Collection is not just of stamps, coins, wines, rocks and all kinds if ribbons, buttons etc. associated with music bands and stars. It could be anything—from tangibles to intangibles. I have collected letters written to me for over 40 years. I love to read letters of over achievers in every walk of life. Of course, I love to write letters so much that I call my spell of letter writing as **Letter Yoga**. Anything, becoming a medium for the union of Self with Supreme, is Yoga.

I picked up a book, an anthology of short stories published in 1945 and two mugs. For all three items, I paid 60 cents—no bargaining! The anthology editor prides himself as a collector, reviewer and writer of short stories for over 40 years! This collection contains 50 stories by 50 writers on the outdoor adventurous spirit of boys, 8-10 years old. Writers range from the Nobel Prize winners to a 16-year old boy.

Americans are the greatest consumers and collectors of items. In life, there is a time to collect things, and then comes a time to disburse them.

(April 28, 2003/Apr, 2011)

BYE BYE MAXY!

Yesterday was a kind of emotional day for me, though it had been in the making for the last couple of days. At 5 PM, I said good bye to Maxy. Patting her on the forehead and shoulders, I said, "You have been good to us all these years. As you now go to a new home of Jamie, be equally good to her." In the same breath, I told Jamie, "Take good care of Maxy. I always took her to Nissan dealerships for regular services, and never parked her in a spot where I myself won't like to stand and wait." In fact, after having seen the valets accelerating cars to park and screeching on the brakes when bringing them back with seats depositioned, I decided not to valet my car. My wife resents my not using valet service.

Three days ago, I cleaned and washed Maxy for the last time. In the morning, my wife and I took pictures with her, and I filled her with premium gasoline. Over the years, every month, I used to take about two hours in washing, waxing, vacuuming it inside and outside. That also provided me a rigorous exercise routine—lasting for almost a week before the stiffness from my shoulders and thighs would go away.

We bought the Nissan Maxima on July 6, 1994, a week after I returned from Malaysia. The entire deal for Maxy was clinched in 30 minutes including its financing! A few days later, I asked the salesman, "How come you accepted our offer without arguing over the sticker price?" "I had sized you up as you walked out of your son's Nissan 300ZX. It was obvious that you liked Nissan. With a computer printout in your hand, I knew you had done a solid homework in checking everything, so why should I waste any time? That is our dealership policy." He summed it up.

Maxy gave trouble free service without ever stranding us in the middle of nowhere. At the end of every trip, I would pat and thank her for bringing us back home safely. Initially, it used to turn my wife off seeing me communicating with a car—like one does with human beings. I tell: Don't the Hindus communicate with their idols of gods every day? At a nano material level, such distinctions between humans and non-humans have been gradually vanishing for me.

Maxy did not have even 82,000 miles. Life is all about memories, and enduring memories are always formed at emotional levels. And, for me, relationships have no more qualitative divisions—whether, between persons, objects, places, and ideas!

(Jan 16, 2004/May, 2011)

COMMENTS

1. It does not upset me that you communicated with Maxy. I have lots of friends who communicate with objects and plants and get good results. Once I had a Tomato plant in my room. I kept it alive for full one year by communicating to it. Normally Tomato plant has a life of few months. I shall start communicating with my objects now. I usually lose ball pens very quickly. Now a days I am communicating with a ball pen gifted to me by a very young girl. Let us see how long it lasts. **Subhash Sood**

2. Dear Bhaisahib, This is one of the amazing things, that we both have common. Whenever I buy my car, we religiously do the complete Pooja with coconut and Ved Shlokas. I agree with you 100% that all this ritual and communication has meaning. I read all your E-mails with full of information, knowledge and the understanding among family, relatives and friends. Kindly keep on sending me your wisdom. With all the regards, Shailendra Bhatnagar

3. Maybe you should have worshipped "Maxy". Hindus also worship their gods. I don't see how you can compare communication with god to talking to a car! One is worship and belief and the other is simply eccentricity. And yes it was a fine machine—your car. Will need some work on the suspension soon though. **Anir.**

WHAT HAVE YOU LEARNT FROM YOUR SPOUSE?

Yesterday, it really impressed me when I watched a husband and wife team of carpenters working at my brother-in-law's house. It was a long weekend project of removing the rotten dry walls of a bathroom, washtub, faucets, and installing new walls and tiles etc. On being introduced that I was a math professor at UNLV, the wife jumped up to tell that she was a computer science major, and currently taking a calculus course! She is a junior in standing with a GPA of 3.7.

It surprised me to see a woman in her late 30s, a full time college student, and working as a carpenter for living—a domain not generally trodden by the US women—forget the Indians. She eventually wants to gets a master's degree in a 'customized' area common to computer science and criminal justice! **Learning never stops for the Americans.**

She was already an exception. Without any reservations in the very first meeting, she told me that she had no child of her own for various health reasons. Her husband had four sons from his first marriage. He looked a 6', 6'' tall gentle giant, and she at 5', 6'' frame a stocky woman wearing a carpenter overall with tools hanging around her waist. She proudly showed me her own tool box. They define the American husband wife team work, diligence and dignity of work.

Assuming that she may have taken on interest in carpentry as a kid while watching her father, I inquired if that was the case. "No, it is my husband who has taught me all about carpentry. I can make any cabinet and do just about any home project." "He must be a very good teacher," I said. "Yes, a great teacher and a very patient man!" **"Teaching a spouse is the most difficult thing."** I remarked, and she nodded.**

On my way back home and reflecting on this piece of conversation, I asked myself; can I specifically name a skill that my wife has taught me. Equally, my wife may have a tough time in identifying what I have taught her after being married for over 40 years. Nevertheless, this is a very important question. To give this question a macro touch, Gandhi's wife called him as her Guru. But it is debatable, whether, Buddha's wife ever accepted him as an enlightened one, since he had deserted her in youthful years.

Jan 25, 2004

COMMENTS

The only difference between man and an animal is INTELLIGENCE. If you wish to expand intelligence you must learn. A true human being keeps n learning till his last moments. Without learning man is an animal or a cabbage. Indians stop learning very soon in life because they are obsessed with money or sex or God. They have no respect for the man who keeps on learning Similarly Indians do not have dignity of labour. I agree America is much more civilized than our old country. **Subhash Sood**

Interesting observation and well written piece. **Inder Singh**

PERSONAL REMARKS

WAKE UP BEFORE NEVER WAKING UP

"Oh, I had just gone to bed!", or "Wanted a bit more of sleep." Such are the usual remarks, whenever my calls wake up friends and relatives snug in their beds. It just triggered, when I called a good friend in Malaysia. At the present pace of life, it is nearly impossible to speak with a person during his/her waking hours. With caller IDs and cell phones, rarely one receives non-business calls, or calls from an unfamiliar phone numbers. This trend has caught over in India too. People only come back to their homes for sleeping. They are desensitized to know how the homes miss them!

I often tease my 60+ year old friends and acquaintances: "Wake up, man, the time for a permanent sleep in nearing!", "Hey, you can enjoy the bonus days of life only, as long as you are awake." Sure, good sleep is a blessing. Sometimes, I may be bluntly frank, when talking about an increasingly common scenario of terminally ill seniors—including the ones with old age. Gently telling, "Why are you running after the doctors for a few hours of lease of life, when his/her mission is already over? Let them go with dignity!" Modern medical system of taking care of Departing ones means spending a chunk of life saving and getting worn-out at the end. The person Goes to Sleep any way. Irony of the whole of illness drama is that while the person was alive, all social dialogues had ceased.

I am one of the rare ones, who call friends as related thoughts flash in. Any planning for a call spoils the mood and pleasure of spontaneity. However, it does pose a timing problem with close ones living in Korea, Malaysia, India and Dubai. No wonder, rarely I get a call from them. Through my **Reflections**, at least, they know what goes on in my mind! Nevertheless, one-way communication does not last very long.

I am usually careful in calling the young ones with small kids. In the fast US life, they rightly need a good sleep and feel rested for the work ahead. But the retirees need to look forward for something else! The first hour of going to bed and the last hour before getting up is a time to stay connected with the universe around. That defines a quality of life. Next time, a near or dear one 'wakes' you up during this twilight hour, say, thanks for calling!

(Sep 04, 2004/Feb, 12)

COMMENTS

I am definitely enjoying your letters, it's worth reading. Your letters wake me up about different aspects of our life and society. Thank you for adding me on your E-Mail list. **Atul Majmudar**

In normal time, as we have these days (i.e. professional work and family responsibilities) sleep is necessary to regain enthusiasm and vigour, and what is normal sleep for one may not be the same for the other. Anxiety, sleeplessness, sensical and non-sensical imaginations of the future of self and family eat away most of our physical and mental energy, and knowingly well this fact we do not take preventive action on ourselves. THANKS FOR THE MAIL. **NIGAM**

Uth jag musafir, bhora wahi, ab raina kahan, jo sowat hai?
Jo sowat hai, woh khowat hai, jo jagat hai, woh pawat hai.—Kabir **Rahul**

Hi Dad, I enjoyed this article. I look forward to receiving calls from you at any hour of the day or night for many more years to come!! **Alex**

ON PHONE CONVERSATIONS

"When are you coming to India?" asked my friend in Patiala, when I surprised him this morning. This generic phrase quickly jumps into a conversation, whenever I call my old friends and acquaintances in India. Despite my gently telling them that they would know of it at an appropriate time; still, it does not register on their minds. There is a degree of excitement during an international call. The voice suddenly goes to a high pitch and so does its volume and the words start coming out in rapid succession.

The overseas phone situation remains amusing for a few minutes. I have 'friends' known for 35-40 years, but we have grown apart over long distances of space and time. It particularly shows up, when they simply keep on repeating that I visit India soon. At one time, I used to drop letters to these friends without expecting a reply. The old-fashioned letters are now antiquated. Nevertheless, *My Reflections* have partly plugged this outlet.

Effective communication (speaking and listening) whether for 10 seconds, or 10 minutes is a cultivated talent. In six years as a toastmaster, I have learnt a lot about it. Essentially, the art lies in consciously cutting the redundancies. For example, when during a phone call, one suddenly inquires about weather that is a sure sign of his running out of news to share with you and/or has no interest in yours. It is time to say bye, bye.

A question may be raised, why do I call such persons again and again? First, they bring a perspective and context to my life. Old friends are like old records, songs and photo albums. You don't go to them every day. However, once in a while, you do enjoy listening and looking at them over a drink. Lots of small memories are tied with them, and they define your persona too.

A paradox of life is that no matter how great are one's past achievements, they begin to look small after a few decades. Old friends are milestones in this journey of life. That is why once in a year or two, I love to surprise my friends in sleepy towns of India. **Pleasure is mine first**. Try it, if you are lucky to have such old time friends!

In the digital age of Skype and Facebook, the word 'friend' is only spelled correctly by the present generation and my generation. I have fewer friends relative to a typical Facebook number; however, my friendships run way deeper. Realistically, my kind of friends may be endangered species. In nutshell, human relationships are reflections of a cultural era.

(Oct 29, 2004/Mar, 2012)

COMMENTS

1. Good friends are like good wine both give euphoria when you need to be high and a "shoulder" when you are down. **Rahul**

2. A good analysis, Bhatnagar Sahib. But do not let your reflections be a substitute for the real calls. **Ved Sharma**

3. At our age we all feel like meeting old friends (specially the childhood friends), knowing their whereabouts and families interacting and hearing our life history and perspectives on issues of the past and current issues of interest to both of us. In fact, there is an intense longing for such people and places of our childhood and younger days (including students and colleagues). **Nigam**

TIME TO TELL A PERSONAL STORY

"I need more volunteers for motivating the kids. We have only 29 speakers for 45 classes having 1700 children." said Joyce Woodhouse, the Director of the **PAYBAC** (acronym for **P**rofessionals **A**nd **Y**outh **B**uilding **A** **C**ommitment). It is a fully funded community partnership program of CCSD (Clark County School District). The speakers are volunteers, and not paid any thing.

My participation goes back to four years when I joined it primarily to hone up my public speaking skills, in addition to being a member of TNT Toastmasters Club. It did not take me long to realize its usefulness. In a subtle way, I was making a difference in the lives of the children. How do I know it? After each lecture, students fill out a comprehensive evaluation on the speaker. During an orientation before going to the classes, the staff tells of instances of how this program has touched the lives over the years.

It is an excellent opportunity for the Indians to tell their communities that they make a difference where they live. **Whereas, volunteerism defines the US society, this concept is foreign to the present culture in India**. By and large, Indians look up for the government for any thing.

There are no qualifications to join **PAYBAC**, except a passion for what you have done, or doing presently. The program is limited to middle schools (grades 6-8) and a few high schools (grades 9-12). One only needs two things; a reasonable command of English and not being shy of standing before the kids. One gets over both after a few visits.

This morning, group of speakers came from police, air force, fire dept, and national companies—like Radio Shack, banks, engineering firms, and a few entrepreneurs and retirees. Mark Alden. a university regent and owner of an accounting firm, took time to be there at 8 AM! In the past, I have seen state senators and assembly persons. Some individuals seen every time I go, since they volunteer 15-20 times a year! I do it 3-4 times. So far, I have not run into an Indian in this program, though Indian kids are noticed in every school. Reason: education is a high priority for the Indians.

Also, through this program, Indians can change the stereotype image of India in the US. The US kids know little about other countries, particularly, India. For instance, today, I was identified from 15 countries besides India!

Irrespective of the subject taught during that hour, it is up to the speaker to inspire the students so that they do not drop out of school. **That is the only mission of the Program.** The reason being, kids, not coming to schools, are likely to create law and order problems.

Moreover, what an infrequent guest speaker tells in a class sticks in the mind deeper than routine lessons. A motivational speaker puts seeds of ideas in the fertile minds during the formative years. Some are bound to become seedlings. Give it a try. Speakers from every background are needed, particularly from medicine that Indians dominate in Las Vegas.

(Feb 10, 2005)

A CROSSROAD OF INDIAN COMMUNITY

There is a clear image of each ethnic community in USA, though it may be debatable. An image is not universal either. The image of Indians in USA is not the same as in the UK, or in neighboring Canada. Images change, but slowly. Nevertheless, a US marketing bottom line is: **Image is every thing!**

The professional image of Indians in the US, as defined during 1960-80, has begun to change. Primarily, it has been due to the migration of unskilled and retired dependents of the first generation of professionals from India. Also, the second generation is more entrepreneurial in every aspect—in taking advantage of the variety of opportunities that this country offers.

Two recent news reports have shaken up the Indian community of Las Vegas. One, 24-year-old Indian woman arrested for prostitution in a casino. An undercover agent apprehended her for selling sex for $500. The second was the arrest of an Indian youth, under 21, involved in a DUI related auto accident that killed the other occupant.

My thoughts naturally went back to 30 years when there were hardly 20 Indians in Las Vegas. Three were in teaching; 3-4 engineers, 4 nurses, three architects, two casino workers, and the rest were in custom tailoring—working out from Honk Kong. There was not even a single medical doctor or a motel owner, when we moved in 1974!

It was about 20 years ago, when we heard of a young Hindu homeless pregnant girl. My wife and were so shocked that we drove around and located her walking dazed along a roadside. She was mentally imbalanced. Besides, immediate help, we even arranged to pay for her airfare to India, and contacted her relatives there.

The point of the story is that we were no less concerned about Indians' image getting a bad rap. Incidentally, that is a survival story too. Las Vegas reminds me of my hometown, Bathinda that was a junction of seven railway lines. The mentally sick persons, thrown out of homes for social stigmas, used to board up the trains. Since every train eventually passed through Bathinda railway station, they would get down and live off the streets for the rest of their lives. Las Vegas, the fastest growing city in the US, has also exploded with Indian population now touching 15,000.

With ample economic opportunities, Indians of every shade of character and profession are moving to Las Vegas. In the skin business, call girls and prostitutes thrive in legal brothels only 50 miles away, or in the casinos under the protection of some employees. The Indian girl caught was perhaps too entrepreneur. Every weekend, youths are caught and killed in auto accidents while driving drunk. Thus, Indian kids can't stay unaffected. The parents overwork at jobs for earning more money, meaning less time for kids.

Fifteen years ago in Las Vegas, it was unheard of an Indian youth living away in an apartment while parents owning a 4-bed room house. It is very trendy today. On the top, there is no holistic influence of religion, particularly of Hinduism. Hindu temples seem to be out of bounds for the Hindu youth, and conversely. On the other hand, the Christian and Mormon churches have youth programs on sex and drug education—besides social gatherings. The Hindu temples have yet to embrace community activities a part of religion.

The point of this **Reflection** is not just to bring a general awareness of the social problems of youth and adults, but also to bring Indian community together to address the issues. The places of worships are ideal to assume new roles and provide supporting environment. The federal government has generous funds to support youth programs. The problems are never eliminated, but can be minimized. A new challenge always opens a door for new opportunities.

(Feb 27, 2005)

COMMENTS

1. Well said, I have nothing to add. In big cities like New York, Chicago, Dallas, Houston, LA, San Jose where the number of Indians are in hundred thousands these incidents are more may be percentage wise same as Las Vegas. But you are right Indians in US still have a very clean image. **Rahul**

2. This reflection should be taken as an eye opener by middle aged Indians who are not in a position to fulfill parental responsibilities, as we think of. At other places in the USA I have seen Indian social, cultural and religious programmes go on frequently and parents take their children for Hindi learning and for participation in such programmes. Some educated (but unemployed) Indian ladies give regular Hindi lessons to Indian kids At Las Vegas, unfortunately, this sort of activity is missing, although a temple has come up. It will be appreciated if Indian kids are given lessons in recitation of religious scripts like *HANUMAN CHALISA*, verses from Geeta, Ramayana, etc. Once this process starts and takes shape most of the Indian Hindus in Las Vegas, I am confident, will come forward and join. Thanks: **NIGAM**

3. One would be dead if one did not have a problem. Problem is essential to keep one alive regardless of what Lao Tse suggests. It is a different matter that I admire him the most. To fight and solve problems is the ground material out of which existence or successful existence or true happiness is made. This is the philosophy of a Warrior. Struggle to improve ones life (even if one has to go to Uncle Sam's country for this) and to improve ones fellow beings' life (as you did when you shipped the Indian homeless female) and few other things are the bedrock of life. On the surface of it we have some points on which we seem to agree. But truly speaking WE CAN NEVER AGREE ON BASIC ISSUES OF LIFE INCLUDING WHAT IS WRONG OR RIGHT AND EVEN THE ISSUE WHETHER IT IS POSSIBLE TO DECIDE WHAT IS WRONG OR RIGHT OR EVEN THE FACT IF IT IS WISE TO CLAIM SUCH A VENTURE IS SENSIBLE. **Subhash**

I wrote: You are right! It also comes to the area of focus; from a point to global when handling an issue in any walk of life.

Subhash: You really know the art of Communication. You can make the other person happy without agreeing.

4. A part of the problem also lies with the fact that the Indian community owns up successes very quickly but when there is a failure around—they are nowhere to be seen. Problems can only be addressed, if we look into our community to identify failures and see the root cause and address them. But that never really happens with us Indians.

Another case in point is that in US life always gives u another chance. u make a mistake—no big deal you can always fix it. But in India if you end up making a mistake in life and there is no way you can redeem yourself. For a simple e.g.: if you blow up your 10th grade exam in India—you pay for it for the rest of your life working in some area which will never pay you money.

5. Very well—I don't' know what to add. **Sibia**

KNOW WHEN TO SLEEP!

Yesterday, a colleague, known for more than 20 years, died in her sleep. She was 67. For those living in youth-driven culture, it is no way to live that old, in the first place. For the ones in their 20s, it was time to go any way. But those who are also in 60s, it was early. It is all relative and depends upon one's focus of awareness!

She appeared in a good health, as only a week ago, she attended a long faculty meeting and later on, signed the graduation papers of her graduate student. Every day, both husband and wife went for an early morning walk. On not finding her out of the bed, the husband went alone. After the walk, when she still was not seen, he found her 'peacefully' dead in her bedroom.

I told my wife that it may happen to one of us one day. At this age, sleep is not easy. Billowed breathing, heaving, snoring and whistling are very common after the age of 50. One spouse, getting the sleep first, keeps the other tossing. The only alternative is to sleep out in another bedroom, if possible. That is what we do, and saw our friends too, who recently visited us.

These days, the only way to catch anyone at home is to call at a time when one is likely to go to bed or leave it. I jokingly tell my senior friends, "The time to go for a permanent sleep is around the corner. Stay awake as long as you can, to share live moments." Those who are of reflective bent of mind take my cajoling remarks in a stride. Others, perhaps, may curse me for disturbing their 'disturbed' sleep. But you keep doing the right thing.

Think of the money, time and energy drained in the hospitals for essentially bringing the 'sleeping' seniors back to waking states. In India, the last religious rituals and traditional home care are disappearing. The trend is to rush them to expensive nursing homes. Who really wants to live when nothing is left to live for a while? Perhaps, a sign should tell it!

In most societies, as the pace of life gets faster, the family size gets smaller. It is not limited to the US. Elderly husbands and wives are seen living alone in metropolitan cities of India too. Then one day, one checks out from the

Planet Earth leaving the other like a destitute. When my mother, father and grandfather took their last breath they were surrounded by their near and dear ones. Each era and culture has its own pluses and minuses on the quality of life. Life comes in a total package.

(May 20, 2005/Apr, 2011)

COMMENTS

1. I do not believe in death, nor do I think of it. I can see that you are mentioning it quite often. I wish you luck in whatever way you think Life continues in the mean time. **Subhash**

I wrote: Contemplation of a thought generates a sequence of Reflections that you have rightly observed. Also, like a physician who stays healthy, but also understands the situation of the sick.

That is my position, like of the Buddha! The dichotomy between life at one end and death at the other is the whole politics of human miseries. They are one!

Subhash: Thanks for understanding. Life can be enjoyed more if death is accepted. It is wrongly believed that death generates misery.

2. *Maut ka ek din muaiyan hai,*
   Neend kyon raat bar nahin aatee!
   Death as its own day already planned,
   Don't know why I can't sleep throughout the night! **Rahul**

AN EMOTIONAL OUTLET

Ageing also means accumulating. And, that could be of any thing—including, knowledge, money, artifacts, diplomas, investments, experiences and memories. I don't know yet about other creatures, but there is no human life that does not stock up things from the day it becomes mindful. Very often, one is subconsciously adding knick-knacks without noticing them. It requires a third eye to observe, as the eyes usually miss objects right in front of them.

A hobby means collecting objects, but not getting paid for it. When one is paid, then it is a profession. These thoughts churned up this morning during a brief 'clean up' spell of my cluttered desk. In a drawer, two 2"x3"tiny address books were lying. One contains full addresses of friends, relatives and acquaintances; all not-so-active. The other address book has active contacts. In the US, no one perhaps uses them anymore. These days, a cell phone, palm pilot, or a laptop carries a zillion of such data.

I myself haven't used these diaries for a couple of years. Earlier, they have traveled with me to many lands. Anything, not periodically attended, becomes inanimate. Now I carry the updated pages of an EXCEL file of addresses. This morning, I decided to trash these diaries. But this very thought also revolted me. Though these diaries hardly occupy any room, but every item does gobble up some space. If left there, and when I am Gone, my kids are just going to trash them with my 'collectables'. This reflection is at least my way of giving these diaries a send-off.

For the last time, I decided to touch the tiny pages containing three addresses per page. A couple of names did not make connections with faces! Once they had impacted enough to get into my diary for a piece of immortality. A few have already Checked Out from Planet Earth. It reminded me of my own mortality. There are quite a few names that have gone out circulation. A funny thing was about home addresses. The speed at which people are changing their homes, phones and e-mails, hard records become useless in a few months.

The human acquaintances are like fruits on a tree—they ripen to various degrees and then begin to fall off naturally, or with slight gusts of wind, or pecks of birds. Over my span of life, these encountered human relationships have touched every shade of emotion. They are funny, full of gratitude and ingratitude, ironic and tragic. These tiny address books have been witness to all of them. It is Time to go!

(June 26, 2005/Mar, 2012)

COMMENTS

1. A timeless reflection. You analogies are so insightful and stir my imagination to thoughts of my own "stuff" and the meanings and emotions that are connected. Some delicious—some tragic. And as you always tell me, that is part of the rhythm and flow of a realistic life. (not your exact words) **Dutchie, now enjoying the fruit**

2. *baazeechaa-e-atfaal hai duniya mere aage hota hai shab-o-roz tamaasha mere aage*
[The world is like children's playground before me
Every day & night, a spectacle unfolds before me.] **Rahul**

3. Bhatnagar Sahib: Mathematics and Philosophy are not that far apart after all. I think many people think and feel the way you do but they do not give expression to these emotions. Some time it is even scary to think openly about these issues. This was a well-written and thought out piece, **Ved P. Sharma**

ON QUANTUM DEGENERATION

Every day that I am at UNLV campus, I can't help looking at the ashwood trees. Each one of them has been withering away. Writing this **Reflection** has been on mind for the longest time. Have I been less sensitive to the state of these trees? I do feel guilty to some extent, but a connection between them and human conditions was not getting clear.

The entire campus has been declared as arboretum for its great variety of flora. Ashwood is pretty much adapted to the local conditions. Its normal life span is 50-60 years, but all of them, growing on the campus, have shorter life. The flaky barks on their trunks and branches do indicate their unhealthy states. Just like a smooth and oily skin is usually identified with a healthy human, the same is true in the plant world!

No matter what time of the year it is, at least, one branch is always found dead. The dry branch could be a big one coming out of the main trunk, secondary, or thirdary offshoot. During the pruning period in winter, the dead branches of each tree are surgically taken off. After the ashwoods are pruned, the blades and equipments are all washed up in antibacterial fluid to stop infection from spreading further. Despite new springtime growth, the Ashwood trees look thinner after each successive year.

It is really painful to watch them during spring months. I know a part of each ashwood tree is not going to get any pinkish green leaves. By April end, brown dead sections are prominent in all ashwoods amidst their green canopies. Once, I saw the entire tree dead in spring! It is like a person dying in sleep, and discovered in the morning.

Last month, I saw an ashwood tree 'known' for 30 years being cut down and its root ball extracted out. 90 % of the tree was already lost. It really hurts, since the disease gradually eats away the tree. On talking with the man in charge of landscaping, I learnt that all the ashwoods on the campus are infested with some bacterial disease. There seems to be no economic treatment! That is why no new ashwoods are planted any more.

It reminds me of lepers on the streets in India. Leprosy affects the nerve endings and essentially starts eating away the extremities of the body limbs. The limbs wither away and are eventually reduced to stubs. It is also called

Hansen's disease. The word leper is derived from Latin, lepra and Greek, lepros—indicating its pre-Biblical existence. When the landscaper was explaining about this specific tree disease I was thinking of it as leprosy of the trees!

(Aug 05, 2005/Mar, 2011)

COMMENTS

Hello Dr. Bhatnagar, Thank you again for your insightful observations. **Arti**

That 'adaptation' may be deceptive. Is that tree native to the Southern Nevada desert? I'm willing to bet it is not . . . . Transplant any plant or animal from its native environment and you are bound to encounter unexpected—and often negative—results. Artificial watering and fertilizing are no substitute for millions of years of evolution!—**Avnish**

FOOD FOR THOUGHT EVERY WHERE

Las Vegas, being the fastest growing city in the US, the households get lot of advertising materials every day. The flyers and inserts are just put in a trash bag before the rest of the mail is brought inside the home. Some free magazines, flourishing on advertisements, are often tossed out too. Once in a while, I turn the pages to get a new perspective on my daily routine. After all, we are remotely connected with everything!

The *Las Vegas Living* is one such free magazine—very beautiful in its printing, layouts and its paper matching the quality of products advertised in it. While turning its pages what caught my attention are the following company pitches:

1. "You didn't pick just any girl . . . . Why give her just any ring?" **Delaria Bros**, Jewelers
2. "Indulge yourself and transform your space into an EXOTIC SANCTUARY" *Riad*
3. "We'll show you how to live in a more beautiful home without changing your address" *Linda Design*
4. "Escape the Ordinary . . . . " **Odyssey, Lighting and Design**
5. "Be original . . . . Be Unique . . . . Be Creative . . . . Drop in and get Inspired" *Design*.
6. "Your VISION is our Goal" *Inspired by Design*

Talking with my brother in law, an attorney, writer and publisher in India, who has moved to the USA nearly five years ago, we both wondered at the production of free magazines in the US. They have irresistible pictures of the models and products. Yet, in the fast pace of life, these magazines are seldom looked at! But someone has figured it out a profitable venture! That is the hallmark of free business enterprise.

My thoughts paralleled my *Reflections*. More than 150 persons, on my mailing list, get them at least once a week. But I have never heard from everyone on any one of my writing products. The comparison stops here. A few more catchy lines are from the same magazine. Just like, in the US, food for stomach is only a few feet away, the signs on billboards, bumper stickers and magazines provide a variety of food for thought!

7. "Husband doesn't do Windows? Get a replacement." *Sun City Replacement Windows*
8. "If You Can Dream It . . . . .We Can Build It" *Reliabuilt Construction*
9. "Paradise Is Closer Than You Think" *Oasis Shade*
10. "Creating a place for life's moments" *Anthony Sylvan Pools*
11. "We Don't Mind Being Stepped on . . ." *Stone Scape Pavers*
12. "Creating the Smile that Defines You" *Distinctive Dentistry*
13. "Give Your Door Some Class . . . . with Glass" *Doorpro, Inc*

That is all in its 132 pages! There are professional writers who think out of these pithy lines in business contexts. For some people, mental tasks are easier than physical ones.

(Nov 10, 2005/Mar, 2012)

COMMENTS

1. In your Milestone #200 Reflection you have come back home—your dear Las Vegas that has proved to be innovative, creative, imaginative in luring innocent people. I am glad you have not succumbed to all those jingles. Yet they chime and ring well. After all, you have found some treasure in the trash or in the magazines that would have seen their fate in the trash bin. **Moorty**

2. Why is that? I can offer 1 reason :—the time period between multiple reflections is too small. By the time a person reads one and thinks about it and responds, another one is already in. Once you slip 1-2, psychologically it is difficult to get to another one. Your reflections are competing against various other things vying for our attention. Though you are higher up on the queue of most people (due to your relationship with them), you are still competing for attention! You are a victim of your own prolific writing. **Vicky**

3. For the record, Uncle, I want to be one of the people you "never have I heard from everyone . . . " I find it easier to exercise the gray matter with your reflections, but I seldom take the time to respond directly. At least with this one (such an auspicious one, at that!), **Sandeep**

OUR BODY PROJECTIONS

"You must be Peppe Sotomayor." I greeted a man sitting on the tailgate of his SUV. "How did you recognize me?" "Because you look like a hiker," I said. It happened last Saturday when I went for a Level 4 hike with Sierra Hiking Club. Peppe is 70, but five hikes a week have naturally tanned his skin. The fine lines on his bronze face capture the fitness and athleticism. I saw it out in a few minutes when he was racing up the slopes that quickly made me windy. But I was feeling pleased in my thought world about identifying a person with his profession or vocation. This is my fun hobby. A general question is: **Is it possible to identify one's profession from his/her appearance?**

The easiest cases are when persons are involved in professions requiring looks and physique. At UNLV, some female students are 'working' girls. It is a term used for call girls—up and down, topless dancers, cocktail waitresses etc. Fully cognizant of the power of their bosoms, low-neck lines, or unbuttoned blouses at the top of full figures, it is a piece of cake to tell what they are good at. Likewise, the big muscled guys working as bouncers and bodyguards are easy to spot. Las Vegas has close to 60,000 young men and women working in the adult entertainment service industry. Of course, tall men are always associated with basketball and solid wide men with linebackers of football.

A few years ago, a survey concluded that Muhammad Ali is the most recognized face in the world. At 6', 5" with charismatic looks even at 64, he still turns the people's heads in any country. It does not apply to men and women who mainly make their living using their intellect. Thirty years ago, speaking with Virginia, an elderly apartment manager, she said, "You must be a physics or math professor." Most Indians coming to the US during the1960s were in academics. It has happened with me a few times. Perhaps, after 45 years, my forehead carries a professorial aura!

By and large, the intellectual prowess does not shine on the billboards that our countenances are. Absent minded professors capture any one engaged in deep intellectual activities. It is fun to explore this question by minimizing the influence of any dress or attire. The muscles of wrestlers from a circuit of Wrestling Mania seem to rip out of their shirts. On the contrary, nerds and geeks are branded with studious work.

The most amazing are the spiritualists. Imagine Pope suddenly taken out of the Vatican in ordinary clothes and is stood on a street crossing. No one would give him a look. It is only when his title, regalia and entourage are with him that he turns into a man closest to God. A spiritual master in one community has little recognition coefficient in any other society. It is only when they speak out and linked with their past and public services that they become venerable. **Essentially, those who live by the looks die by their looks, and for the rest of us, face recognition is a zero sum game**.

(March 02, 2006)

JOURNEYS OF LIFE

"How come you are also not going?", asked our 18-year old college-going granddaughter, when she came to know that my wife was going alone to spend a few days with our son in California. I simply said, "That is how we often travel." I was cognizant of the fact that she observed it for the first time, and may have felt strange about us not going together. The TV shows have made the US as the most stereotyped society in the world.

Of all the human relationships the one between husband and wife is the longest and most engaging in every facet of life. If there is an ultimate experience of intimacy of the body, then it is certainly here. For mind experiences, it provides a playground, but only in rare cases, it is for the ultimate soul encounters. In recent times, Gandhi and Kasturba realized all three in each other at different stages of their lives. Amongst the founders of organized religions, Buddha had it at the body plane only. Jesus had none. Mohammad had all three too, though with different wives.

Two months ago, when my wife was visiting her sister in Chicago, I jokingly remarked, "How come you are not spending 2-3 weeks with her?" She took it, as if she was not wanted here. Afterwards, my time line took me back to Patiala days in May 1968 when we were only married for five years. Due to my weird job circumstances, I agreed to my wife visiting her uncle in Mumbai with our 3-year old daughter. However, I compelled her to return to Patiala after only two days! It was crazy of me then, as it is now. She had reached there after 36-hour of tiring train journey. But it did prove that she was missed!

There is no end to explanations for such spousal behaviors. But the reality is how we deal with them. Since we are often inquired, I jocularly tell that we are like the top army generals, who are instructed against group travels so that in the event of a tragedy, at least one survives. In a serious vein, I tell that it is convenient for the hosts particularly in Indian living conditions to accommodate the singles than doubles. I remember back in India before the 1960s, six guests spending a night in a one-room accommodation. But hospitality is changing in India, as the US life styles are impacting all over.

However, there is a deeper aspect in our relationship; we frequently need more space. Both of us being the eldest in families of seven siblings each, we had our formative years molded the way we wanted—not being aware of its merits and demerits. Like any thing is life, what reaches a height also falls down.

As the couples near 70, a lot more is familiar than the unexplored territory in each other! I told my wife that the US iconic image of husband and wife sitting on rocking chairs and not talking with each other means that their communication is taking place in silence! They have arrived at a blissful stage. The Hindu *Ashram* (system of life) recognizes this stage in life. The divorces and marriage breakdowns after 50 years of age may be looked as an entry into the third phase of life called *Vanprastha Ashram* (away from the family and more towards the society)!

(Feb 17, 2007)

COMMENTS

1. What an excuse of not traveling with your wife. Actually in US the couples in their golden age share more, travel more and do more vacationing then they did when they were younger. There are statistics to prove my point. I for one do not buy your explanation and I bet neither did your 18-year-old granddaughter. **Rahul**

2. Divorce can be Vanprastha if divorcing parties have loving relationship. **Subhash**

3. Thanks—wonderful words of wisdom. **Hortense**

4. Mohammad had an intellectual connection with his wife? **Anjali**

5. Dear Satish, I thank you for this reflection. After 40 years being married to Norman Slater, I reflect upon that experience as the most tremendous reward and true happiness vehicle for me. Love, **Dutchie**

PERSONAL REMARKS

A BITE FOR THE SOUL

Long human associations with friends and relatives, in particular, are formed early in life. Their memories begin to crystallize around the age of 8 years. By a **Principle of Symmetry** of life cycle, these bonds begin to de-crystallize during the last 8-10 years of life span. The story with ideas, being unemotional, is different. It starts with maturity of mind and only fades away when the mind loosens its grip independent of time frame.

The psychology of association struck me a few days ago, when I called my younger brother in India. By the way, India calling is no longer that expensive, as it used to be when I came to the US forty years ago (AT&T charged @ $5/minute with advance booking; not person-to-person!). The overseas conversations used to get jumpy in the sense that we touched upon as many bases as possible. It is in contrast with Unlimited Free Minutes available in the US during weekends for the cell phone users. Now, I love to chat for 30-40 minutes bringing out details of a topic while stretching the vocal cords.

During the call, my younger brother suddenly remarked, "Remember, once you refused to give me Rs 20!" This incident may have happened 40 years ago, and I wondered at him holding this 'grudge' for so long. Having no recollection of it, neither I wanted to argue with him nor remind him of scores of good deeds that my wife and I had done to him and his family. At age 60+, he may have felt strangely 'relieved' after unloading it on me. Incidentally, this kind of blunt talking is typical amongst the Indians.

For a few minutes, my mind kept swirling around and it gave an unpleasant feeling. But it changed quickly. It was a moment to examine the psychological contents of my mind. I recalled close friends and relatives, who years ago, had hurt me that I had been nursing to balance those equations. However, today, I gave them a benefit that they may not even remember the incidents, as I don't remember this Rs 20 one. There is a saying in life: let it go or let the sleeping dogs lie. Settling an old score out is like removing a scab formed over a cut. The wound still being green, without a scab healing will never take place.

This turned out to be a great mental exercise—an inner catharsis. My mood changed immediately. It was not a pious forgiveness or overlooking his faults. Actually, it was coupled with realization. By actuarial tables, our days are numbered, so why to snap years-old ties over trivialities. I felt sorry for my brother. As a matter of fact, the blood ties begin to get thinner after the age of 50, unless they are continually nourished with common ideals and missions in life.

Hey, this is not a saintly act—nevertheless, an inner transformation on a micro scale. However, if I am hurt again on the same spot by the same person, then I equally believe in straightening the person out.

(May 02, 2007)

COMMENTS

1. *Jo Mil Gayaa Usii Ko Muqaddar Samajh Liyaa*
   Jo Kho Gayaa Mai.N Usako Bhulaataa Chalaa Gayaa
   Gam Aur Khushii Me Na Fark Na Mahasuus Ho Jahaa.
   Main Dil Ko Us Muqaam Pe Laataa Chalaa Gayaa **Rahul**

2. Hi Satish: I was answering some messages from both our sons, David at Holloman and Derrick up in Portland and happened to see your message. Very well said. I have been using the computer so I am sure Bob has not had time to read it or comment. Actually, I came to this place of reflection about 35 years ago. Bob's dear mother ALWAYS brought up past hurts and injustices and it was so clear that life was way too short to indulge in such things. She would also tell me something that I had done, or Bob had done to hurt her, JUST before she left especially if she was flying out, just as she went through the boarding doors. I was quite fond of her so it hurt, but was also a lesson to let things go. I especially like your analogy of the scab and taking it off does not allow the wound to heal. Good reminder. Fondly, **Marilyn** Moore

3. I could really relate to the final line of your piece—I have a current situation which it reminds me of. Take care, **Hortense**

4. I never understood why there is such "blunt talking" within the Indian community. Not just the community, but within families. American families are constantly in disarray, and I think it is a result of the role-playing on national television. In the early nineties, television centered around family oriented programs; for example, Cosby, Family Matters, etc. The idea was that children, who did not have a parent at home, could learn basic values and morals from these programs. It is sad, but when parents are struggling with two jobs they do not have the opportunity to nurture their child. Now it seems the new television is all about finding every possible twist and chaotic event in life. People are now obsessed with chaos and I believe they indirectly model their own lives based these programs.

Is it possible that we here in the US are trying our hardest to maintain tradition and Indian culture? While in India, culture and tradition is leaving the homes within commercialized areas. Maybe they too are being affected by the chaos illustrated on television. **Sundeep Srivastava**

5. Respected Bhai Sahib, Namaste. Only two days back, We all family members were at dining table and in relation to a topic being discussed, I told Mani/Ashi and all others that we should always remembers and quote one's gestures done for you in your past life and brush aside the memory of any bitter feelings, may be for any reasons towards someone. This keeps your mind positive and peaceful. Yesterday, I read your close reflection containing the revival of a bitter event relating to 45 years past period. I was really surprised that is it possible that during this long span of 45 years, nothing good was done to that person/his family and how could one forget all the positive gestures and store the memory of only bitter event that too of a very trivial nature. I think it reflects only the culture of one's nature which can hardly be changed at such a ripe stage of life. **Vinod**

6. The inner workings of another's mind are always a mystery to outsiders. There is no possible avenue to travel to explore the thoughts, emotions and intellect of another, even a close sibling. I've had to live with many mysteries and Oh, I didn't mean to send that one at this time. Time was needed to refine my thoughts. Sorry I pushed the wrong key. Love, **Dutchie**

LIVING AT 81

Certain days leave indelible marks on the psyche. At times, one tends to think that all days are same, but it is the acuteness of observation that distinguishes them apart. Today, within a span of 12 hours, the lives of two 81-year old persons have impacted me. To anyone in the 60s, active persons in their 80s arouse inspiration, envy and jealousy, since various physical and mental infirmities envelope vast majority of octogenarians.

My sister has known an 81-year old lady, who *thinks mathematically*. Incidentally, it is the subliminal theme of all math courses that I teach. In the afternoon, we were introduced on the phone, and thus spoke for a while. Naturally, I was curious about her interest in mathematics that, I found, was simply her way of life. 2500 years ago, Pythagoras said that the natural numbers hold the key to the mysteries of the universe, but her vocabulary included differential equations, formulas and functions!

Sometimes, the professionals in mathematics go to extremes in their views about people who do not know hardcore mathematics. If persons like her were lawmakers and university regents, it would be so easy to get support for science and mathematics. She was a professional dancer till the age of 45. While conversing with her, I understood the technological greatness of the US. Nowhere else in the world, general pubic appreciates mathematics, as in the US, which naturally tops the world in science and mathematics.

In the evening, I was bowled over by the 81-year old comedian, Don Rickles. It was my first comedy show, and I wanted to see how nimble he was. He gyrated, rocked, rolled, kicked the air, dropped and picked up the mike, and paced all over the stage. He kept the audience hilarious for 60 minutes—non-stop! No matter where a showroom seat is, my binoculars are always there. I had them focused on his robust, square face with a bit of skin hanging under the chin. But he was not out of breath! He did sip drinks a few times.

No two world-class comedians are alike, though a dozen mathematicians may work on the same research problems. However, no one wants to hear the same jokes again even from the same comedian! Comedic originality is very high. Don Rickles is known as the **Sultan of Insults**. People pay to laugh, when 'insulted' by him! In the show, he made joked about Irish, Jews, Blacks,

Japanese, Italians, Jesus, Popes (new and old), Phillipino, Japanese, Puerto Rican, Mexican and Polish. But he did not make fun of the Muslims!

I have been in the US for nearly 40 years, but I am not a fan of any particular singer or a comedian. Music and comedy are subtle and cultural, and I still miss nuances and the punch lines. It is different with my kids raised here. But my purpose was solely and purely to watch an 81-year old man swaying a crowd with his talent. As I was driving back home at midnight, I said to myself, that one should continue to pursue a path where one excels. That is one secret of a productive life, and that makes an ordinary life extraordinary. What a Day! I had no idea of it, when started it off in the morning.

(May 27, 2007)

COMMENTS

1. Yes, we "oldsters" are a hardy, robust and active bunch. Our resiliency is extra ordinary. We do all that gyrating with gusto. Being in the 80's, therefore, is not to fear. We laugh at all you silly youngsters as being wimpy. Ha ha ha ha . . . . Thanks for the reports about your life, experiences and philosophies. **Dutchie**

2. Dear Bhatnagar Sahib, First of all I must thank Vinod for asking you to put me on your mailing list to receive your e-mails, secondly, my profound thanks to you for sharing your ideas with me. I agree with your statement expressed in your recent e-mail that one should continue to pursue a path where one excels . . . . and then an ordinary life becomes extraordinary. I am personally convinced after teaching for 38 years at Newman University that teaching profession is second to none, however, my son and daughter argue that practice of medicine is second to none (since both being physicians). As I teach, young people grow and change in front of my eyes. Being a teacher is almost like witnessing human birth, especially that moment when newborn begins to breathe. Nothing is more fascinating than being nearby when the breathing begins. Likewise, for me nothing is more exciting than to witness than to witness human minds blossom!

I continue to remain eager and impatient in carrying on teaching and research with same fervor and enthusiasm I started out 38 years ago. I thank God every day for His help in making me choose teaching profession. Dear Bhatnagar sahib, have a great summer. Please convey my warmest regards and love to your younger brother and sister-in-law. Sincerely, **Surendra Singh**

ROUND TWO OF BIRTHDAYS

"Continue the celebration of your birthday (B'Day) for one more day," said I, while greeting my sister-in-law a day later. Coming from India recently and being over 60, hers was a lamenting response, "Bhaisab, one more year of life is gone!" Promptly I added that is all the more reason to celebrate a few years that are now left. **B'Days must be celebrated at both short ends of life.**

A life is defined by its perspective—like, glass half-empty or half full. The mind can perceive only one state at a time. But this B'Day thought has been taking me for a ride. Why people celebrate B'Days? An infant has no sense of a B'Day before turning 4 years. Our 2-year old grandson just loves to blow the candles out every day, as if his B'Day!

The crux lies in our hopes in the life of an infant. All the homeless, Hitlers and Buddhas were once pretty infants for their parents. The parents live their dreams, unfilled aspirations, and want to leave a legacy through their kids too. Hope continues to multiply as the child goes from nursery to school to college, but it begins to decline after 40!

For a person over 60 years, who is hoping for his/her rosy future? **Hope is an emotional investment.** Assuming, the parents are still alive, they have already shifted their capital from their children to grandchildren! The world only cares if you do something for it!

B'Days parties are a mark of affluent societies. As a kid, on my B'Days in Bathinda, I wore new clothes. Mother would invite the family priest for blessings. The atmosphere of the entire house felt spiritual on B'Days. By the teen years, I started revolting against my B'Day. Mother did not insist, as she had six younger kids to go for them.

My wife is very high on B'Days—whether it is hers, or of kids, relatives or friends. She loves parties and celebrations. I don't remember any B'Day party before age 50. But I have diaries filled with notes on such days. For years, writing a journal on B'Day and NY day was a ritual. One of these days, I will bring their highlights out into my *Reflections*.

Throughout my years in 40s, I believed that life is to be lived in a manner that others emulate and celebrate your B'Days—being a kind of famous. I consciously never worked for it. However, when I turned 50, a memorable B'Day party was combined with our son's graduation, and his going away for the officer training in the US Army Reserve.

Excessive deprivation in life's experiences is inimical to the life itself. Life is enriched and it becomes inspiring when its experiences are shared. Otherwise, the world would never know if one ever had any experiences. Memories are not tangibles like material goods. The world nibbles out the tangible assets. It is the right spread that matters. **Nevertheless, you are alive as long as your B'Days are celebrated!**

(July 13, 2007)

COMMENTS

1. Mostly I enjoy, as I also told you earlier, your reflections which I read carefully. **BSY**

2. Very apt observations. To remain as optimistic as possible, try to philosophize on what others have which we are not fortunate enough, realizing that no one has it all, be grateful for what we do have .... in short contentment and a dedication to some cause beyond our personal life is the key to happiness. Very human to forget!! Regards. **RAJA**

POLISHING DEFINES LIFE

Sometimes, a sequence of things, completed one at a time, can end up quite amusing and illuminating. This afternoon, I decided to buff up a leather document case before giving it away as present. It is brand new, but was tucked away on the top of a closet over a year. The odor of leather polish, being like that of a cigarette smoke, can waft over the objects. So, I carried the polish kit out in the side alley of the house and settled down for work.

For the first time, I noticed a sponge applicator. Yes, I had bought it myself a year or two ago, but had never put it to use! After the Kiwi leather lotion was carefully applied, its directions were to leave it for several minutes for the chemicals to penetrate. Instead of waiting it out, I went inside and brought out my hardy summer sandals for a 'facelift'.

Suddenly, I was transposed back to my days in Bathinda (BTI), my hometown in India. Polishing the shoes (usually one pair to wear) was a Sunday ritual. The dust, grime and knockouts received daily equaled to the ones faced in a year in any US town. Here, the shoe uppers never crack up, un-stitch, or dissole. While holding up, I examined the sandals for any cut, tear, or excessive grazing from the edges. With a scrubbing brush, I washed the outer soles, knowing that soon after, they would be banging the pavements.

While polishing, I re-lived some 50-year old moments. Sunday, the 1-day weekend, seemed to last longer than 24 hours! Besides shoe polishing, I used to clean up my bike—one spoke at a time, rim, and oiled the parts. It was a Raleigh bicycle, the only one in BTI then! Taking care of the objects, you ride on, is an extension of taking care of your body and mind! The topmost fun was an hour—long full body massage with mustard oil. It was a part of the culture of the region. I still do it at least once a week. Early in the morning, we would go for an outdoor activity, have a hearty breakfast and heavy lunch that may scare my US raised kids today for the fat content. Yet, we were mostly skinny, but wiry.

In contrast, the 2-day weekend in the US is never long enough. It seems to vanish while sitting in front of a screen/monitor, talking on phone, or driving around. These time guzzlers did not exist in BTI then, and I try to minimalize them in Las Vegas, my hometown in USA. However, life comes in packages—you can't always pick and choose.

After I finished polishing, I felt good despite the toxic substance that may have gone into my system. Polishing means looking closely at an aspect of life. Everything, that takes good care of us, is usually taken for granted— whether they are our shoes, feet, close friends and parents! There is a merit in having shoes polished at a shoeshine box, body massaged in a spa, or car waxed up at an auto wash. Polishing dusty relationships, once in a while, is the most enduring exercise!

I am now a product of two intellectual cultures, a connoisseur of the two, and hopefully one day, they would shine out of me!

(Aug 15, 2007)

COMMENTS

1. Dear Satish, One, of many, best words in this one is "shine." It is rarely used these days. Yes, shinning and shine help to make me smile. Thanks for these thoughts. And, keep 'em coming. Very insightful and delightful. Hugs, **Dutchie**

2. This one is very good! Like your point of view and the trip down memory lane. I too used to do the Sunday shoe polishing routine when I was in school. **Anir**

3. *Aataa hai Yaad Mujh ko Guzara hua Zamanaa*
   Wo Baagh ki Bahaarein wo sab ka Chah-Chahanaa
   Aazaadiyan kahan wo ab apne Ghonsle ki
   Apni Khushi se aanaa apani Khushi se jana
   Lagti ho Chot Dil per, Ataa hai Yaad jis dam
   Shabnam ke Aansuuon per Kaliyon ka Muskuranaa
   Wo Pyaari Pyaari Surat, wo Kamini si Murat
   Aabaad jis ke Dam se tha Mera Aashiyanaa (Iqbal) **Rahul**

4. Hi Satish: Bravo! How you have converted a simple chore into a reflection bringing out the two lifestyles and cultures and how our past lives amidst us. **Moorty**

5. Nice insights; but I thought you would have noted the obvious connection between the terms 'polish' and 'reflection' . . . literal and otherwise! **Avnish**

6. Yes. Polishing dusty relationship is the most enduring sort of exercise. I liked the use of the metaphor . . . one of my habits is after my bath I recite a prayer in my mind. 'O Lord, just as I cleaned my body, pl. clean my heart too . . . ' It has a very positive effect . . . I think. **Abraham**

USELESS UNTIL FOUND USEFUL

Certain days are unbelievable and become naturally unforgettable. A week ago, while going up a hill to see Neemuch Mata (local goddess) Temple, I ran into a person coming down. At my greetings, he stopped. He carried a small shoulder bag containing several flyers and booklets about the organizations he founded many years ago. Being known to my co-walker, I learnt that he was Dr Agarwal, a nationally known figure of Udaipur.

Dr Agarwal, now 78, is a retired professor of oncology and surgery. His one-man crusade is against tobacco use in every form. Casually, I inquired, "Does tobacco really have no use to anyone for any malady?" Emphatically, he said, NO! Giving him another shot, I said for years, the serum in poisonous snakes had no use. However, it is now used for several medicinal purposes. In a southern state of India, deadly snakes are farmed for their serum. But the crusader, Dr Agarwal, was firm about his conviction. He showed me a flyer of the cancerous problems caused by tobacco chewing. Excess of everything is bad—sooner or later. After handshakes, we resumed our trails in opposite directions.

Tobacco is a unique plant. It may not be growing in every country of the world, but there is no country where it is not intaken in a certain form. Personally, I smoked cigarettes for several years; initially, not more two a day. Gradually, it increased to 8-10 cigarettes in a chain and then none for a week, or so. It went on for a few years till the urge to smoke was gone by itself. I am certain that my smoking was a natural response when my brain signaled a low level of a particular chemical compound found in the tobacco.

An hour later, I narrated this incident to my brother-in-law, who knew Dr Agarwal. On Agarwal's position on all harmful effects of tobacco, he told me a story of his long suffering with a stomach problem during his 20s. After undergoing several unsuccessful treatments, a house remedy—a pinch of tobacco, was recommend after a meal. In a few days, the chromic gastentroligical problem disappeared. He continues to use it daily. He is 83 years—not on any medication for BP, diabetes, etc. He is devoutly religious, physically fit and mentally sharp. Is it a magic of daily pinch of tobacco?

In less than two hours, this tobacco encounter became a metaphor of life. Nothing is useless for everyone. Also, no one thing is useful for everyone for all the time. The chaos changes into order; the noise changes into a meaningful signal. **All it requires a good research**. My wife, a lover of greenery, hates the barren mountains of Nevada. I told her once that for millennia, they were useless. But since 1895, they have provided the world tones of gold, silver and other minerals—used in every aspect of life.

This approach applies to ideas, ideologies, institutions, and places. There is a purpose of everything. It is a corollary of *Advaitya* of Shankaracharya, **Unified Field Theory** of Einstein, or **Principle of Oneness**.

(Dec 09, 2007/India)

TIME TO TAKE TIME!

About a week ago, I caught Anna, my nephrologist daughter-in-law, on the phone. These days, it is not easy to talk with a person on a phone. A new reality of modern life is that there are more phones than inmates in a house! The modern technology that lets one speak with a person on the other side of the globe can also cut a person out, if unwanted at a given moment.

In a typical rush-rush life style, Anna appeared wrapped up. Yet, she asked, "What is new?" Generic questions—like this, "How is everybody?", "How is the weather?" are vacuous in terms of closeness and enrichment that a conversation should breed and bring out, once in a while.

Trying to bring her 'closer' to the present, I said, "Anna, February has been a very big month for you!" On sensing her unbelieving, I slowly listed the following events for her:

1. Your mother is visiting you from east coast for a month. It is a mutual blessing these days.
2. Avnish is leaving NASA, the best government agency for Goggles, the best amongst the private companies.
3. After years in medical college, residency, fellowship, part timing and moonlighting, you are going to work full time with a nephrologists group of your choice and place.
4. On the Valentine Day, your daughter completes two years!
5. You have bought a million dollar home of your choice; all done within this month!
6. Above all, February is your birth month. This day should top it off.
7. The sale of the old house and transition has been very quick, painless and seamless!

Speaking of homes, years ago, someone differentiated between a home and a house. Home is described as a physical structure. House includes people, furnishings and emotional environment etc. Incidentally, the Webster does not make a distinction between the two!

In a fast paced life, whether in the US or erstwhile sleepy countries like India, there is no time to wallow in grief or stay high on one's success. If hit by a tragedy, the loneliness and job pressure would force you to be out of it by pill, will, or kill. Pills for anti-depressant. Will to grab life by the horns and move on. Kill; yourself by suicide or in carnage as increasingly reported. Some 'psychologists' have described such massacres as paranoid bonding with the society at large!

There is a strange anatomy of grief and joy. Sorrow expands and engulfs when continuously dwelled upon. But it dissipates on being shared. Chekhov, a great Russian short story writer describes the global permeation of a coachman's grief over his son's sudden demise. On the contrary, happiness quickly diminishes to a vanishing point, if not shared with anyone. It multiples when shared with others. My mother also used to do spend money through grandkids and small acts of charity. It brings an element of social spirituality to people around.

If life is a gift, then being fully cognizant of it, is sacrosanct. In public speaking, the right pauses enhance the effects of a message. For enjoyment in life, the pauses are essential in fast routines.

(Feb 18, 2008)

COMMENTS

I agree, pauses are necessary. I like this line particularly nana!—On the contrary, happiness quickly diminishes to a vanishing point, if not shared with anyone. It multiples when shared with others. **Anjali**

TIRED, TIRED, TIRED . . . . !

"I am not feeling good," responded my 16-year old grandson, when I called him around 9 AM for a morning outing. The more I persuaded him, the shoddier became his reasons—like "I am tired", "feeling sick" etc, etc. As a concerned grandfather and personally health conscious, I said, "Your health worries me. At this age, you should be jumping all the time." I want him in physical shape before his first solo travels in Southeast Asia for a week during spring break.

Often, I see 6-7 grandkids in my extended family in Las Vegas. The most common refrain during family gatherings and conversations is that kids are not feeling good. It is paradoxical statement, since the kids do not have adult like feelings in the first place! Feelings are cultivated socially. Also, there is hormonal connection. For instance, watch any TV show, featuring 1-4 year old children, one hears, "Time for the baby to sleep", "Baby does not look good." The expression, "Put the baby to sleep" ignites me, as it stirs a morbid scenario of a veterinarian putting a sick pet to Sleep forever.

Raising children is the most important phase in a civilized society for its continued survival. At the same time, in history, both barbarians and Spartans, with their rough and tumble approach on physical development alone since infancy, have built great empires. Years ago, some anthropologists predicted the extinction of a certain tribe in Andaman and Nicobar islands in Indian Ocean. It does not matter how their newly-borns are raised today! It sounds spooky.

I am at least two generations apart in reflecting on this aspect. Lots of things have changed where I grew up in India—now living in the US. Last night, my 78-year old neighbor recalled her life in Boston 70 years ago—room radiators were run by a coal stove in the basement ignited every evening; the kids played on the streets in snow. Rarely school kids got sick en mass, as it happens today. The rosy cheeks of the white kids have disappeared! Paleness is synonymous with sedentary routines.

The have-to-have-this-too life style has been pushing parents to longer and staggered working days on multiple jobs. The tired parents would naturally see fatigue in their kids too. It is painful to see kids treated like pieces of furniture. Kids, quietly watching the videos and TV alone, give the parents time to 'relax'. The sedentary life styles of the last 50 years in the US and of ten years in the middle class families in India have weakened the foundations of new generations.

The common fatigue syndrome is essentially due to disusing of the legs. The weariness is not only at physical and mental levels, but at spiritual too. Unfortunately, the recourse is on medication—popping of the pills. Circulating blood-carrying oxygen to the brain brings cheerfulness. One hundred vertical jumps while standing at one place, or jogging a mile does wonder in ten minutes.

Two days ago, it was alarming to read that this year's flu has spread to 49 out of 50 states! Getting sick has become a norm rather than an exception. My students demand make-ups for missing classes due to illness. At semester-end, I ask them, did I miss any class? There must be something right in my life style. **Life follows a principle of conservation of practices**. The present day kids may be gaining something living mostly indoors—while losing what we leant playing outdoors.

(Feb 24, 2008)

COMMENTS

1. I hear a lot fatigue complaints around here too. I do not remember saying or feeling fatigued at that age. You are right again. Legs are not used. Things come easy. No great urge to work for things. **Ved P. Sharma** (Economics Prof and Chair, 69)

2. A sad result of increased technology . . . . And the walk to school and back home every day was a joy in that we talked and thought and mentally prepared for the classes while gaining more strength in our legs and lungs. Snow, rain, sleet, mud, sun, wind whatever . . . . we walked. One minor correction: we had central heat through radiators in each room which were heated from a coal furnace in the basement of the apartments. We always lived in apartments, never had a house until I was married for three years. Thanks to the Veterans Administration guaranteed loans for WW II veterans. I am so happy that you keep me on your mailing list. Hugs, **Dutchie**

GARAGE SALES MEAN RECYCLING

The events of a certain day leave a lingering fragrance. Yesterday, it started with neighborhood garage sale. For the last several years, the housing management company has been advertising neighborhood garage sales each spring and fall. It captures the proverbial American phrases: Spring Cleaning and Christmas Shopping. People lay out goods for sale in their driveways. Often, friends and family members, living close by, also join with their items. It then turns into block gatherings for enjoying the outdoors as well. Hundreds of people are drawn in. Some set their sales up by 6 AM, and it goes on till either things are sold, or one gets tired of waiting.

I enjoy browsing the garage sales. It is nice to say hello to the neighbors living in the community. Our association has 750 homes. Americans are the friendliest people with strangers. It is due to the fast pace of US life styles that does not let emotional closeness take any roots. During the sale, I had conversations on topics from math/theater classes to radio talk show hosts.

At one time, I was embarrassed about being seen in garage sales. It came from a culture I grew up in India of the1950s. For instance, we used apparels to their last threads. That meant only the discards for give-aways. Imagine, people still accepting them in India! American capitalism and consumerism have turned homes into small museums and warehouses. The freshness of the indoor air is sucked out by the goods—leaving the inmates chronically ills with various ailments.

Amongst the ten books bought, four are in *Chicken Soup Series*. Yesterday, a relative happened to meet after many years. The *Chicken Soup on Parenting Soul* was presented to him. It was perfect, as his widowed mother in her 70s had moved with him, and his married kids are ready for parenting. That is generally how my books get re-circulated. The best buy is NBA picture book for coffee table. The write-ups and pictures are so inspiring! The basketball game, an American invention, is a metaphor, a window of life for those who pour their souls into it.

It was funny that I was driving my small Mercedes while stopping to peer into the garage sales. I could sense people reacting at this sight. Of course, people are seen getting off their expensive cars and haggling over prices in garage sales. Most likely, the un-sold stuff is going to be dumped in the trash next morning. So, it is the best place to bargain, or strike a deal!

One stop had two beautiful landscape oil paintings. I hesitated to inquire the price, as there were no stickers. However, having visited many art galleries, something was noticeably special about them. The man, in 50s, appeared somber. I cracked his veneer by commenting on a 4'x6' painting in clear plastic cover standing against the jamb. Only five were done 35 years ago, and he had paid $1000 for one! Watch for surprises in garage sales, as no two are alike.

It was fun and educational. Besides books, I look for baseball caps and mugs. Two brand new Gevalia mugs with golden trims and logos were for 25 cents apiece! A woman put out her entire collection of bean-stuffed toys and furry animals. Sales are driven by boredom, newness, deaths, divorces and moves. In life, attachment and detachment are two sides of the same coin!

(May 18, 2008)

COMMENTS

1. Oh, you've captured the essence of garage sales. Congratulations. This was fun to read and moved along smoothly. Hugs, **Dutchie**

PERSONAL REMARKS

TESTING & STRETCHING LIMITS

Three days ago, I safely returned from Bolivia after spending a wintry week at heights between 12,000'-14,000'. The time was spent in a region covering present Bolivia and Peru (South America) It was mainly around Lake Titicaca, the largest lake in the world—at an altitude of 12,500'. Because of the fresh water, several civilizations have flourished there since the BC era. The trip was neither for any hike nor spiritual exploration. It was essentially educational. We were a group of 16 college teachers, across the US—all curious about regional archaeology, culture and astronomy. It was a Chautauqua course, run by the University of Texas at Austin.

We flew in and out of La Paz (means **Peace**), the highest capital city in the world, populated by 2.2 million people. At an elevation of 12,000', it is nestled in a canyon, but not as spectacular as Grand Canyon of the US. Its airport, at 13,500', 30-minute away from the city, is the highest commercial airport in the world. I never encountered so many firsts of the world in a short time!

Talking of heights, Lhasa, the capital of Tibet, is at altitude of 12,000'. But it cannot challenge La Paz since Tibet is not a free country. China, finding India not strong enough after its independence in 1947, militarily annexed it in 1951. In 1962, it occupied nearly a million square km of India's territory. Bolivia too has lost its eastern region to Chile and southern to Paraguay. Incidentally, the average height of Tibetan plateau, the largest in the world, is 16,000'.

Whereas, the human body is amazingly adaptive to rigorous physical conditions, it is softened by climate controlled modern life styles. With airline flights, one can go from sea levels to highest elevations in a few hours. It is very risky for the sedentaries and out-of-shape people since the glandular adjustments may not be that quick. In our group, the age ranged from 40-70 years.

For the first two days, we sipped cups of coca tea (banned in the US!) and walked around leisurely. A quick difference in breathing was noticed during morning *Pranayam* exercises—one exercise, done for 120 seconds in Las Vegas, could not be sustained for 20 seconds. However, on the third day, we walked early morning for nearly three hours at an elevation of 13,000'.

Often my steps were heavy and I used to find myself trudging at the end. But without stopping, I tried to acclimatize my 'under-developed' lungs with thin air. Once, for about 4-5 minutes, I gasped for air by breathing from mouth— not a good sign, when the nose breathing goes out of gears. But a little rest stabilized it. Oxygen was available in most places, but I did not go for it. This experience is worth it. One reason being, that I still have aspirations to go to an ultimate pilgrimage to Mt. Kailash (21,800') and Manasrover (Lake, at 15,000'), in Tibet region! During this Olympic Year, the Chinese authorities have denied pilgrimage visas to all the Americans.

Life is all about living at its fringes. Generally, the physical limits are optimized by age in the 20s. Intellectual limits can be extended through the 50s. However, certain 'mental' and 'spiritual' faculties continue to expand even in the 80s. **It is in the limiting experience alone, the moments of self-realization, or the glimpses of eternity shine out**.

(June 26, 2008)

COMMENTS

Dr. Bhatnagar, This was really an interesting read! Singers often feel the effects of altitude changes when visiting other cities and are advised to arrive several days before any singing engagement. Recently, I visited Santa Fe (altitude 7040 ft.) and felt quite a difference, so I can only imagine 12000 ft! Anyhow, I am currently working for International Game Technology as a business analyst (fancy for management consultant) for the gaming industry. It is certainly an eye-opener and a great deal of work (and fun!). Hope you are doing well. Best. **Renato**

III.   MUNDANE (Global)

GANDHI REMEMBERED

Yesterday, when I read of the rampage of Kishore Kumar musical night at Berkeley, as reported in the *India West* of Sept 21, I wondered how long this Hindu-Sikh communal hysteria is going to continue. It reminded me of a line in *Julius Caesar*, a Shakespearean play. After having whipped the emotions of the masses with his rhetoric, Antony was asked what course this hate rebellion would now take. He replied: The dogs of war are on afoot. Antony meant, thereby, that it was easier to start an uprising than control it. It is like a fire, which can be easily ignited, but not easily put out.

Presently, Punjab is caught in communal tension. Fortunately, this has not spilled over to other Indian states where the Sikhs and non-Sikhs are not disrupting each other's joyous occasions. But how this hatred has crossed the oceans to reach the US and Canada has to be studied. Similar disruptions have been reported from New York and Chicago also.

In 1947, at the time of India's partition, Punjab and Bengal witnessed unprecedented communal frenzy in which innocent men, women and children were massacred in the name of religion and new nations. For a while, it appeared, as if the destruction of life and property was never going to stop. Every kind of political appeal to stop the human carnage went unheeded. Then comes this frail man on the scene, about whom Einstein had remarked: Coming generations would find it difficult to believe that there ever lived a man in flesh and blood.

Gandhi went on fast unto death. He just could not see the killings of the innocent on the top of India being subdivided against his very best wishes and efforts. For the first few days violence continued because of the momentum it had gained. But as his condition began to deteriorate, his message of non-violence and communal harmony began getting across. By the end of the month, when there was little hope of his remaining alive that total peace was restored in Bengal, and Punjab was quiet too. Thus, he clearly demonstrated that one man can stop a hate campaign and put the flames of violence out.

Some two hundred countries celebrate Gandhi's birthday. But, let we, the Indians in the US, do it in a more pragmatic way. Let another musical night be organized in the same hall. Mr. Patel has suffered a financial loss, and I appeal Indian community and their friends to support Mr. Patel not only morally, but financially too for putting that kind of show again. Let the hecklers try to disrupt it again. It will be a test of Gandhian moral force to bring about a change of heart. Irrespective of the outcomes, Indians would pay a living tribute to the principles of non-violence that Gandhi lived and died for.

(Oct 02, 1984, Gandhi's Birthday)

DEATH MEASURES LIFE

Yesterday, I had a unique experience of watching a Sri Lankan film, **_Pura Handa Kaluwara (Death on a Full Moon Day)_**. It is in Sinhalese language that I have no familiarity with, as I grew up in Punjab. The film copy did not even have English subtitles. However, the event organizer, in his introductory remarks, said that the powerful visual images of the movie would offset the absence of subtitles.

Being a member of Asian Studies Committee and International Film Club at UNLV, I was invited to be on the panel discussion after the movie was over. The panel included the award winning and popular actor Joe Abeyawickrema visiting from Sri Lanka—besides two local Sri Lankans. The movie was produced in 1997, but was banned by the Sri Lankan Government. After a four-year battle, the Director Vithanage won its release from the Supreme Court. Since then, it has won several international awards.

During the panel discussion, I found out that my comprehension of the story was reasonably close except of the dramatic climax at the end. It is the story of the impact of a young man's death in Sri Lankan civil war. It shows how the tragedy shakes his sisters, old father and other community members, when his dead body is brought to the village. In my panel remarks, I said, "Death stops life around it. The brothers and sisters cannot accept it in their hysteria. The parents are either shocked into outbursts, or frozen into a silent rage. Community life, around death, slows down with grief grinding life into mortality. Thus, one can measure the quality of life by the radius in which community life around death comes to a standstill—for a while."

Growing up in Bathinda, I recall till the 1950s, the social mourners publicly wailing their way to the house of the deceased for days. Presently, amongst most Hindus until the 13th day of mourning has passed with final rites, the sadness and gloom pervade the air. On the contrary, life today in the USA is so fast paced and disconnected that neither there is time for a prolonged celebration of a joyous occasion, nor time to wallow in grief over tragedy. The pressures of high-tech life are so high that one is simply forced to clean up and pick up the remaining threads of life just after a few hours. I also added, "The ability of an individual, family or society at large to get back to normalcy is equally a sign of its vitality and love for life."

Here is a paradox. A great life in death tends to halt the life around it, but the dynamics of forces, in a great society, push the life out from the depth of its sorrow. I think that is where the life of a martyr is distinguishably epitomized. Only a week ago, I watched a recent film production on the life of **Shaheed Bhagat Singh**. The energy and electricity that his death brought in Indian national life seventy years ago can be felt even today while watching its movie!

(June 23, 2002/Aug, 2011)

WINE, WOMEN AND SCHOLARSHIP

Amidst this gala, it flashed my mind—what if a blind folded young man (at heart or mind) is brought in this huge ballroom decked with crystal chandeliers on panted ceilings, colorful wall and carpet coverings, spot lighting and live band music, and suddenly his blind folds are removed, then how is he going to react to an atmosphere where wines are being served all over along with an array of cheese and cold cuts. Snacks and fruits are artistically carved and laid out on several central locations. Above all, throngs of women flaunting their wares—bare backs, midriffs with navel rings, shapely legs, and pants so below the waist line that little is left for imagination. It is a riot of deep and long cleavages, firm and wobbly bosoms—all daring men to ogle with doubly intoxicant looks. Black dresses whether on the whites or blacks accentuate the skin. **It is a small paradise on earth, where one can have all sensory delights!**

If this scenario has to take place any where in the world, then it has to be in USA. And, if it has to be in the USA with a touch and style, and within the reach of every one, then it must be in **Las Vegas, the Adult Capital of the World!** That is how I felt it last year and that is exactly how I feel at this moment—an hour after returning from this annual event billed as **UNLVino**, a festival of 1000+ wines tasting with a theme **"Take a Sip for Scholarship"**. Last year, I let this moment slip before I could capture the ethereal, sensory and sensual experiences. I am determined to do full justice to it this year.

UNLVino had a humble beginning in 1975, a year after I joined UNLV. It has the world famous College of Hotel Administration, where students come from at least 50 countries every year. This event started as a wine tasting evening with the support of local wine dealers for raising money for scholarships. Soon after, it moved to a large warehouse of a wine distributor near famous Las Vegas Strip. Its popularity rising exponentially every year, the event moved to the 20,000-seat basketball arena on UNLV campus. But as popularity caught the fancy of Las Vegas tourists, it was moved to a central location in Bally Hotel and Casino. But for the last 3-4 years, it has been held in a 50,000 sq. ft. ballroom of Paris Hotel and Casino. During these years the admission has gone up—from $5 to $35! However, the entire proceeds go to UNLV scholarship fund. It is a management mark of student volunteers and nearly 100 business sponsors!

The Paris Hotel is built completely on the theme of Paris, France—associated with the latest in fashions, wines and arts. Housing UNLVino in Paris is perfect match. From 12 to 3 PM, the event is restricted to special guests of casino industry, UNLV and wine industry. It is thrown open to the general public from 3—6 PM. My brother in law, being a casino executive, we were there around 2 PM when the line for 3 PM was already 100 men deep! I can't imagine taking any alcohol before noon. UNLV student volunteers were there at every step from checking the minimum age of 21 years and directing traffic, as pockets of crowds would swell up.

As soon as you enter the ballroom you are given a wine tasting glass—designed with UNLVino logo 30 years ago. One may pick up a free wine notebook of 250 pages that lists all the wines, description of **ten** wine tasting tips (**Sugar level, Acidity, Tannin, Fruit Intensity, Gas Presence, Wood, Alcohol Level, Body/Texture, Varietal Character, and Balance**), evaluation categories, and a point system. Additionally, each wine may be evaluated according to individual's own criteria. The piles of wine notebooks, magazines and pens truly make it an educational delight.

But who is in a mood to read it and then go for a sip? Here are sample descriptions of some wines: "The intense aroma jumps out of the glass and envelops you with its seductive perfume. The palate rejoices in the silky flavors of plums, black cherries and mushrooms", "a full-bodied wine, opulent with flavor and grace", "an homage to Madame Pommery, this wine is pure, refined, sublime, and sensual". Incidentally, the name of this wine is Pommery Brut Louise.

Being a little fired up, I immediately went up to the nearest booth. It is after gulping the first one down that I looked it in the book! I have lost a little patience for notes now. In the past, I used to make notes on each wine that I tasted and tried to sip as many as possible! Can you imagine any one tasting even 100+ wines? **It is man's ultimate fancy to have a taste of maximum number of wines and women!** Irony is that man is not made for any multiplicity of actions, but he keeps shooting for a thousand in his mind! **Wine only increases man's desire for a woman, as Shakespeare put it**.

UNLVino is a place to see and be seen. Society being transient and the city touristy, it is difficult to know who is who in a flux of a thousand crowd. I was told by a political acquaintance that the US Senator John Ensign was there. Of course, UNLV police officers were seen in their full black regalia for people to notice their presence. They were not looking at any one. **Men, wine and women form a very combustible material.** In fact, a lot of women are hookers. Do I recognize them; no way? It is from the police reports, that on a given weekend some 15,000 prostitutes, call girls and hookers descend upon Las Vegas. The women alone know the art of separating man from his money!

There are no chairs where you can sit and sip, otherwise, no one will leave the place voluntarily. It is all standing atmosphere, and you stay in motion for a new sample of wine and snack. There was a station for desserts and coffee for people to consume before driving back home. Caffeine neutralizes some alcoholic effect. As a matter of fact, a company, called, **Designated Driver, Inc,** arranged rides for tipsy persons to their homes along with their cars.

A popular feature of the evening is wine auction. That is not my type of wine interest as some wine bottles are auctioned off for a couple thousand dollars! There is a history behind some wine bottles. In all there were 52 kinds of wines in various sizes up for auctioneering. Wine is not what most Indians consider *SHARAB*, a lesser kind of drink. **Wines define not only a society, but sometimes, a civilization**. Shiraz is the most popular name given to a wine, no matter what part of the world it comes from. It does not come from the present Islamic Shiraz in Iran, but from a 2500 year old Persian Civilization that perfected its wines, and Shiraz was a seat of its power.

Well, we spent three heavenly hours. If a Mughal poet could achieve a piece of immortality by his verses on the beauty of Kashmir Valley that he called it a heaven on earth, then I certainly have earned my piece of immortality today. All you have to do is to visit Paris, Las Vegas next year!

(April 26, 2003/Feb, 2012)

MY GRAND DAUGHTER SHERNI

Sherni (means lioness) is a nickname that I always use to address my granddaughter (daughter's daughter) Anjali (means hands cupped for an offering). It is a separate narrative how this nickname, out of many names that I gave her, has stuck around. She likes it too! In a few days, she will be 15. It has been my custom lately to make birthdays special with an additional gift of some **Reflection** on the life that intersects with mine.

I have seen Anjali grow from the moment of her birth. During the first four years, my wife took care of her while our daughter decided to do her second degree in school teaching. My earliest association was to take her out in the backyard or on a neighborhood street whenever she was a bit cranky or upset. The best way to reset the mood of a child is to disconnect it from its little environment. So even when she was a few months old, I would immediately carry her out, get her closer to leaves, twigs and flowers, and make her touch, hold and pluck them. She would just forget about crying.

One day, I called little sparrows to come to us. There was no way sparrows would respond to my calls. But for little Anjali, calling sparrows became a real fun. We would say, "Come sparrows come; Sherni is calling you, and so on." Sometimes we would throw some food crumbs and seeds to attract them. This continued whether we were in backyard or on street. At times, passers-by would wonder at our callings. But lo and behold, after only a few weeks, the sparrows started flying in our backyard from all over. They perhaps got conditioned to our calls, no less than attracted to food crumbs.

As Anjali started walking, I would prompt her go near the sparrows. I really noted some nice characteristics about them. **The main thing is that the capability of bird's brain is inversely proportional to its peanut size.** The sparrows never let me come closer than 4-5 feet, though I was the one giving them food. However, little Anjali would be walking amidst them. They felt fully at ease with her. But they would read intentions in my eyes that I was trying to hold them in my hands. They would flutter and fly way from me. At times, they would even let Anjali's small fingers caress their feathers. One day, **I told my wife that, in general, sparrows are far smarter than American girls**. It is so easy to entice girls with any promise of jewelry and fun. No way, can one do it to sparrows even in a few months. Sparrows really test you out.

I do not have such early memories of my maternal grandfather. My memory goes back to 1945, when I was ready to start schooling. And that is where he played a formative role in my life. He taught me Urdu and English languages at home that gave me a head start in school. He was very meticulous and time bound in his routines. Daily, he would get up at 4 AM and walk for at least three hours seven days a week—rain or shine. He never cut short on his time even when his knees were so bad that he could hardly get out of the bed. During the last days of his life, he used to walk one mile in three hours! Now that I am in my 60s, I find myself walking at any time of the day. During younger days, I found walking very boring, as I associated it with ageing. I liked running and doing hundreds of push-ups and sit-ups, and later on, took on weight lifting and yoga *aasans*.

Another thing that I picked up from my grand father is oil massage. We, the kids, and our maternal uncle would take turns to rub oil on his body twice a week. During those days, mustard oil was the only oil available for everything—whether massaging or cooking. In the US, I can claim to have massaged my body with every available oil.

A strange thing is about the way humans learn in life. One may not learn every thing what parents and teachers are consciously trying to drill. In due course of time, when I try to analyze why I do certain things and the way I do, then it turns out there is always an individual who unknowingly made some impressions on me. It is a story of human race. After the age of 50, we quote our parents more often than we quote holy Scriptures.

For the last 2-3 years, I have been getting both my grandchildren into tennis. Anjali has become a good player and can play on her school team, if her mother would let her balance academics and athletics. Also, I play with them a mind game, named, **Phone Jeopardy**. It was more fun for them till a couple of years ago. I would call them after returning from work, and check on their school day and homework. Then each one would choose an area of his/her interest, like any sport, spellings, geography, history, etc. Then, I ask questions worth a nickel, dime or quarter—depending upon the challenge. For 20-30 minutes, it was quite an exercise for me to think of questions, and fun for them to win some change. It expanded their awareness beyond the confines of school.

I know Anjali has arrived at a point in her life when gradually she would be absorbed by people and activities outside the orbits of parents and grandparents. That is how life is enriched. I was very fortunate to have lived with my maternal grandfather. He reservedly delighted in my success in school and college. That was an era in India when humility was a great virtue. Acclamation was not trivialized on the youngsters, as seen in the US today. Here self-esteem is never enough. There is a golden mean of the two. Sherni, I am so happy to have you as my granddaughter. Incidentally, I knew my own grandfather for 15 years! Happy Birthday to you!

(May 02, 2003/May, 2011)

BURIAL AND SURGERY OF PET PLANTS

Have you ever seen, heard a tree committing suicide, getting paralyzed, or meeting a slow death? An hour ago, I got back into the house after what in the US, people would call spring-cleaning of plants. It is not pruning done during winter, when there is no flow of sap from the ground roots to up—the crown of the tree. A couple of days ago, my wife declared, "If these dead rose bushes are not dug out soon, then I am going to pay someone do it, as they bother me." I am against paying for such house chores, as I like to do a little labor for its therapeutic value.

I have special relationships with these plants. A diary is kept of all the plants in the front and back of the house—with periodic notes on their progress. Each plant is associated with some family occasion and events—like visit of a nephew or brother. Three rose bushes that died have a very strange story. Our front yard has cacti on one side of the driveway and red boulders and rocks on the other. Our neighbor had a grassy lawn. One day, I observed his water sprinklers wetting our side of the yard. In order not to let water go waste, I planted rose bushes and water resistant plants and cypress trees along the common boundary. They all did great. Let me add, that I had buried our sprinklers under the rocks when I decided to be in tune with natural desert setting of Las Vegas area.

Back tracking a bit, we bought this house about the same time, when our neighbor did it. After the divorce, wife left and the man was rarely seen. Two years ago, he told me that he loved our desert landscape so much that he was going to turn his grassy lawn into one like ours! What a vindication and applause for which I hardly lift a finger! He was also tired of paying for the maintenance of the lawn. I said to myself. "Oh, that knells the demise of my plants!" That is exactly what has happened in the past two years. Call it my lethargy, or my love for hardy plants; despite my declaration that I was going to revive a line of drip system to water those plants, I never did it.

Water resistant bushes, being hardy, are doing fine. Three rose bushes and three cypress trees had a slow death. And I witnessed it. First, you watch lower parts of stems getting dark red; after a year the whole bush turns charcoal color and is gone. There being no root balls, it did not take even two digs of the pickaxe to yank them out. I felt the ground was not willing to let them go. **Time creates an attachment between any two objects.** My emotional state was well past, I piled them up on the curb for the garbage collectors.

Cypress is a stately tree erect and tapering like a ballet dancer. Even when three of them were clinically dead, I did not feel like digging them out. Their little brush leaves have turned all brown. I argued if some one does not know the original color of the cypress trees, then the dead trees still look fine and blend into the reddish landscape. Actually, I bought a can of flaming red paint for spraying these cypress trees, but have not sprayed as a gust of wind may not return the paint spray back over me!

Pyracantha, a tree like bush, suffered from a definite kind of paralysis. Very clearly, one could see that one of the two major trunks of the bush was dead. However, the other half is pretty healthy and blooming. So while at this cleaning project, I decided to do some surgical work on it by just cutting the dead part of the trunk. I had no way of going to the roots and trace its dead sections, as the brain surgeon do it in treating brain disorders, particularly in epileptic cases, in order to control seizures.

While doing the spadework, as a byproduct, I had a good exercise and sunbath!

(May 04, 2003/Apr, 2011)

PERSONAL REMARKS

WALKING THROUGH A CEMETERY

This morning, I was in a cemetery. In fact, I am drawn towards it once in 2—3 months. Being two miles away from home, it falls within my walking orbits. My wife knows it. I don't talk about it, as it makes people nervous—going there without a 'purpose'. The nearby one is called Palm Mortuary and Memorial Park. It covers an area of at least 100 acres. I enter through one gate and go out of the other—perhaps, symbolizing a journey of the soul!

My gait unknowingly slows down the moment I am inside the Park. Hardly any human is seen. But somehow, I am mindful of a multitude of souls. Thoughts on mortality and immortality always surface up. Despite the fact that the human frame is perpetually changing, its Ultimate mortality drives home only in a cemetery, when you are all alone. Immortality, whatever it means, recedes away. It forces a reality check on life.

I read the carvings on the tombstones—all kinds of names, dates of births and deaths. Walking by them, I calculate life spans. The manicured grassy lawns with flowers placed in flower holders on tombstones paint a unique sight. You just don't see it anywhere else! Sections of the Park have various names. For instance, **Garden of Honor** is for defense veterans. There is one section where 1-2 persons are already buried, and the adjoining plots are waiting! Recently, the company has created high profile burial enclosures. They are like special boxes in sport arenas, where the rich can indulge in other pleasures while watching live events. **Life is a business from its birth to burial, and nowhere is it more evident than in the US funeral industry**.

The dignity and respect toward the dead, in a cemetery, is a socio-cultural phenomenon. It reminds me of a recent comment by Secretary of State, Colin Powell, when he was questioned in England by the Archbishop of Canterbury on the US intentions on the occupation of Iraq. He said, "Over the years, the United States has sent many of its fine young men and women into great peril to fight for the freedom beyond our borders. The only amount of land we have ever asked for in return is enough to bury those that did not return." It threw a pall of silence.

Generally, while walking around, I also do various upper body stretching exercises. They just stop in the Park, as my awareness is stretched there. **I feel like a point in an endless continuum, yet having potential to influence the universe—thus living the *Principle of Butterfly Effect*!**

(July 26, 2003/May, 2011)

LOST PLEASURE OF WALKING

For me, walking is like masticating of thoughts. It is time to sort out ideas and unclog the mind. Every time, I visit India, I notice cities increasingly choked with unbridled construction. The villages are deserted, as the poor, in particular, are leaving for supposedly greener pastures in cites. The urban traffic is growing exponentially while streets hardly improve. Dust and noise pollution are playing havoc with public health. It is unpleasant to walk any time any where, as fear lingers that a vehicle may knock you down from any side. Walking is becoming a dying past time in urban India.

In most US cities one has to simply step out of the door of a house or hotel and walk in any direction. By law, safe and wide side walks are provided in city neighborhoods. Within a mile of any residence, grounds of neighborhood elementary school are always open for walking. But it is not easy in old Indian cities—like Bathinda and Ambala where the inner streets just cannot be widened.

I have no fixed time for walking, and do it on an impulse to get away from the roof above me. It may happen after sitting at a PC/TV or doing some reading, writing for a couple of hours. Yes, sometimes a home argument also drives me out! Any time between 7 AM to 11 PM is fine. In India, there is no leisure walking, once the sun has come up.

Traffic blows the dust high up and over, that trees are laden with white powder. Greenery is not seen anywhere. Last year, I saw items in an attic covered with drapes to save them from the daily onslaught of fine dust getting at the fourth floor of a high rise building.

Today, I compulsively left home around 10 AM and walked in the bylanes in order to avoid heavy traffic on major roads. I had a cap on the head, and a hanky covering my mouth and nose. From the looks of people, I felt out of place in my own hometown, but could not take them off. **The humans get used to every kind of pollution, and that is how new life strains metamorphose**. I walked for more than two hours with a few stops. I had enough of walking for a day, so got into a rickshaw to get back home.

Thoughts were racing up in my mind at the paradox of life. In the US, streets are wide and side walks clean yet seldom have I noticed any one walking. Yes, besides a couple in their 70s, I am the only regular walker in the neighborhood. Everyone recognizes me. I realized it when I walked door to door in an election campaign last year. In the US, walking for the young makes no sense, whereas, loitering is a crime! In India, youth is hardly seen in any athletic activity—forget 'boring' walks.

I have inherited some walking genes. My maternal grandfather was gone out walking from 4-8 AM. He would rest for an hour at his joints before returning home. A walking bug pushes me out. **Walking is certainly therapeutic, and for me meditative**.

(Nov 13, 2003/Feb, 2012 (India))

COMMENTS

1. Your thoughts are important. You bring out the problems of our citizens here, lethargy and forgetting about the future. Walking on a golf course is a distinct pleasure. The open spaces, the trees, bushes, flowers, grasses and birds are beautiful and calming. Even if I don't play golf, just walk the course the experience is good for me in many ways, mostly "calming."
   Dutchie

2. Dear Bhatnagar, Warm Greetings. I enjoyed all your e-mail articles. I feel that U are opening a genre in literature, call it electro-literature. I simply walked along the article when you visited your native place in India. I felt that I was one in the audience. Your young and energetic picture 30yrs back still linkers afresh in my mind. I don't know How U look now. Your flashy smile and twinkling eyes excite me still. Your article on walking made me remember the experience I had in Bloomington. To burn of my sugar, I used to walk for an hour every day in the morning in Bloomington. I also enjoy your article on "The Marathon Race". So, keep it on. I am your patron. **Soori**

MAKING THE TWO ENDS OF LIFE MEET

This morning two things happened! While jogging around the block, as my first activity of the day, I stopped by the house of an Indian neighbor. Seeing their four-year-old son in a warm-up suit, I asked him to job along with me. The parents were a little hesitant that the kid might bother me or just run wild. Applauding that the kid was not sitting in front of the TV like a zombie, I encouraged them to let him go outdoors.

Yes, the kid was excited to be out. I showed him how to avoid icy patches on the sidewalk and stay on the street while watching for traffic. We walked, jogged and small talked for 15-20 minutes before bringing him back. My thoughts flew out for the legendary brave Spartans who used to place their newly born males out in the open for a day. If the baby died, then it was considered not fit for combat—but was fully nourished, if he survived the endurance test.

Our son's in-laws, visiting us these days, have a rented car to see places around. They are in their mid 60s and planned one-day trip to LA. But their daughter, living in Davis, California has cancelled it. While being pregnant, she is overly concerned about her father's driving and mother's allergies. Twice a day, she checks on their activities. Last June, while visiting Davis, I decided to bike to the university campus 6-7 miles away. My son, a bit apprehensive about my riding a bike at 60+ said, "Dad, take the cell phone and call me when you are there." Smilingly, I took the phone that I seldom carry. For a moment, I relished his concern that I had it for him when he was 4-5 years old!

With ageing, physical reflexes do slow down, but the reflexes slow down faster, if the elders are discouraged from staying active. Recently, a friend told me about the death of his father at 99, who immigrated to USA at the age of 70. In LA, he drove sporty cars, lived in an apartment by himself, and enjoyed a slate of activities. During the last 2-3 years, his motor skills were not as fast as LA traffic. Essentially, he called it QUITS in the arms of his oldest daughter whom he had cradled up in his younger days.

Life is cyclic. As babies, our first 2-3 years of life are fully dependent on others. Likewise, as elders, our last 2-3 years of life are fully dependent on others. Pediatrics and geriatrics are called upon at each phase of life. All infant caretakers become young caregivers, who eventually become old caretakers! It is a perennial law of human nature.

Does this principle apply in the universe of birds and animals? My observations tell me, no. Birds and animals instinctively learn all tricks of survival. But once the babies are able to fend for themselves, they are gone! None takes care of the aging parents in the world of birds and animals. Yet, we hardly run into dead birds and animals in a forest when out for a hike etc. Human beings are unique in this respect. Or, is the human race alone 'domesticated'? Ironically, the pet birds and animals share the same infirmities of infancy and old age, as do their human owners!

Dec 18, 2003/May, 2011

COMMENTS

All about caregivers and caretakers! How much of this "perennial law of human nature" is genetic or instinctive and how much is social or conditioned — one wonders. Did Mother Nature while creating 'life' distinguish between different living forms? Or all living species are just different manifestations of the same life energy? — These differences acquired during their journey on earth — but journey to where?

Well, we don't come across old, disabled and deficient animals, birds and insects in the forest — they are just eliminated by the grand natural process called 'survival of the fittest'. **Competition is the norm.** At the same time we find old, disabled and deficient taken care of in the so called most brutal species — hyenas (wild dogs of Africa) for example, not to talk about social elephants. **Co-operation is not that unknown.** While highlighting the deficiencies of his faculties the keen observant once said, "Life is a master paradox". Care for the young ones, yes we find in all species. But we do find instances of cannibalism even among 'higher' like chimpanzees — that too by the female energy of that species! Some say even we have lived as cannibals in our chequered past. And who says we are not now? CMC would sound a good acronym for a modern business enterprise but if we expand the same it could well mean "Cannibal Multinational Corporation". Packaging is an art we excel in. Everything nicely packed sells well.

Leaving the topic of care and cared let me introduce myself. I am Raman Mittal, Dr. Nirmla's son. Presently I am living in Delhi where I work at the Indian Law Institute. I have enjoyed reading your thoughts which you have painstakingly typed down and very kindly send to some others including me. Last time I visited Chandigarh; I took a printout of the mails and handed the same to my mother who has replied you via regular mail. Many thanks for your mails which vibrate with living thought and fond emotion. With kind regards, **Raman**

Child is the father of the man. Actually there are few species in animal world which take of old. This is seen in animals, which travel in herds. **Rahul**

PERSONAL COMMENTS

A KIND OF PARK

Your thoughts are not completely yours—they are functions of an environment too. Being on the phone for nearly two hours, I stepped out for a long walk around at 11 AM—just to breathe fresh air. I followed my footsteps, and they were following some drummer inside me. They eyes were only passive observers. Suddenly, I became aware of the boundary wall of the Palm Memorial Park. Yes, it is a place of every kind of burial (the dead are 'parked' here) right in the heart of the city. The park has manicured lawns with sections named—Garden of Reflection and Garden of Resurrection etc. Being Saturday, friends and relatives of the Departed ones were visiting the burial plots and walls. The place was dotted with flowers, real and unreal—but both indistinguishable!

The Hindus and Sikhs cremate their deads. The cremation site is called **SHAMSHAAN GHAT** (place of the dead) or **RAMBAAG (Garden of Rama).** Lord Rama mostly led a life in grief—first, when Sita, his wife, was in Ravana's custody for 13 years, and later on, when he was compelled to banish her from his palaces. Since at any time of the day, one would find piles of smoldering fires over the dead, such a site is usually on the outskirts of a town. At night, it is believed to be a joint of the ghosts. As kids, we used to play pranks on each other by daring to go there at night.

As I grow up, lot my ideas have undergone changes. But it is constant for the disposal of the dead body. I like my body be cremated without any rituals as soon as I am dead without any prolonged support system. These days, one can choose a day and place of delivery of a baby, but no one can openly choose a time and place of one's death. The great *Rishis* supposedly do it. In the western society, it may amount to an assisted murder or suicide—both illegal! I love cruises, so what if I am Gone on an ocean liner? In that case, let my body be tossed out in the ocean—consigned to the water grave, as it is called.

In the US, cremation is no less expensive. A few months ago, a friend died in Las Vegas. With the simplest casket for cremation, memorial service in the park and preparation of the body for viewing, it cost the family nearly $7000. Flying the body to India alone would have cost $7,000! It is rightly said that in the US neither birth nor death comes cheap. No wonder—the young couples are heard saying that 'we can't afford a baby'!

Such were my thoughts, as I would stop and go at various burial plots. According to tombstones engravings, only one man was noticed to have lived for over 100 years! I have no idea of his legacy—never heard of him on TV/radio, or read in a newspaper/book. There was a famous line of Helen Keller on a tombstone, 'what you have deeply loved is never lost'. In a memorial park, you softly greet visitors, and move on. The park is within my walking beat of three miles. My younger brother once told me how he decided against buying a very nice home facing a park that in daytime turned out to be a memorial park!

Jan 03, 2004/May, 2011

COMMENTS

1. *umr bhar dekhaa kiye marne kii raah **ma**r gaye par dekhiye dikhlaye ge kyaa* (**Mirza Ghalib**) **Rahul**

2. For years my wish has been to be cremated, . . . but after 3 days so the soul has time to depart. Many people do not want to buy homes by cemeteries, (memorial parks), while others declare how quiet it will be, no neighbors to bother them with noise, parking, etc. To each his own . . . that's why I love real estate! Blessings and have a wonderful day! **Renee Riendeau**

3. Mata Ji has left the body (at 92). I shall answer your e-mail later. **Subhash Sood**

I have not yet fully come out of effects of the loss of my mother. I agree to what you say most peoples' thoughts are decided by environments. There are MANY WHO CAN DECIDE TIME AND PLACE OF DEATH. There IS A TECHNIQUE OF IT Dayanand and L Ron Hubbard among others decided it. This is one of my goals. **Subhash Sood** (Died of a stroke three years later)

A STAR IS BORN!

Yesterday night, my brother-in-law called to know about my deeper feelings on my becoming a paternal grandfather. I had nothing specific to say. But he kept pressing on it that the question registered on my mind. He is a deep thinker. Amongst the Hindus, there are a lot of myths and legends about begetting son of a son. Five days ago, I was indeed delighted on getting the news of his birth. It has added another bonding to life.

An enigma is often observed in human life. There is a universal jubilation at the birth of a child. Why? A baby is like a start-up company, and people put their faith/stock in his/her future that he/she may bring them security and prosperity in one form or the other. It all lies in hope. At the other end of the spectrum, a man completing a journey of his life is an open book. Instead of hope, it is the legacy—good or bad that publicly stands out.

While driving to the office this afternoon, I saw a panhandler in his 40s standing on a crossing. I suddenly visualized him as a son—born to some parents, years ago! No parents ever dream of such a future for their children. Yet, there are millions of beggars. Last night, a colleague told me how he disconnected all the ties with his only child, a son of 37 years. He migrated from Bulgaria and earned his PhD. But the son drifted away to the lowest denominator in US life.

A legend of Buddha tells, while he was still in mother's womb, the royal astrologers predicted that either he would be a great king, or an eminent seer. During his upbringing, the father king did his best to keep the son into the materialistic way of life. But, one midnight, the son permanently walked out and away from the palace life. Years later, he became Buddha, the Enlightened One.

The Hindu view of a son carrying on his parents' legacy is myopic. It puts a burden on a child to become what he may not be programmed by his genes. Also, it is a fallacy to assume that only the parents' genes determine the course of a child's life. The scientific fact is that the genetics traits can be triggered by genes even 50 generations removed! Various environments, where a child is raised, also influence the shape of life.

My thoughts took an inward turn. When I begot my son, my father was 61. He may have seen my son only on 3-4 different occasions, as my wife and children left India before my son was one year old. My father was never to see his son and grandson again, as after two years he himself became a star in the firmament of a heaven. What is my longevity after seeing my grandson at 64? Personally, I put it at 36!

The elation at the birth of a child is a projection of our beliefs and actions. It adds a new dimension and a purpose to life. The name chosen for my grandson is Arman—meaning desire. Living up to the meaning of my name, Satish, has been the purpose of my life. Arman, I wish you live up to the meaning of your name, once you become aware of it!

(Jan 25, 2004/May, 2011)

COMMENTS

A very enjoyable essay! I, too plan to live to be 100! Renee means reborn . . . I love it and have many re-born experiences in my life . . . planning to have many, many more. I have six grandchildren from 3 to 20 and have been able to be with my daughters the first week after every one of them was born. Birth is truly a miracle . . . **Renee** Riendeau

CONGRATULATIONS! **Wadhwa (Died in Nov 2004)**

This one is very well written. **Aniruddha**

Between a doctor mother and a NASA father' and a Math grandfather' he will shine like a star. **Bob/Baldev Singh**.

Your writings stimulate me to think. I'm grateful to you for sending them along. **Dutchie**

Congratulation Grandpa; It will be for you to contribute to development of your grandson, if the opportunity comes your way. **Subhash Sood**

Thoughtfully written . . . as usual. We always talk about how a child is molded by genetics, parents, environment, etc. But I've always been fascinated about the reverse influence a child has on those around him. As a new parent, I witness this first-hand. Neither the most respected rulers nor the most feared dictators possess a fraction of the power that a 6 lb infant effortlessly exerts on the human heart & mind. What won't we do to elicit even the smallest smile from a baby? What won't a parent sacrifice for the well-being and happiness of their offspring? Some will argue that such intrinsic bonds are biologically hard coded in our brains to promote the survivability of our species. But I think they're there to promote self-awareness. As the poem that Gori sent expresses, "The day you were born . . . I stared at you in awe until I wasn't sure which one of us had just been born." **Avnish**

TIME IS MANAGING US

"Bring your calendar at the meeting." "What!" I responded to a committee secretary yesterday. Then she explained that I should know my engagements so that dates and times of future meetings are fixed up, when I come at the first meeting of a 25-member committee. Being in a new position of the Associate Dean, I have to attend several meetings with people and in areas not familiar with. It is a learning experience and that also makes the job interesting. At times, an appointment does slip out if not properly entered in the calendar and/or registered on mind.

Time is the most precious commodity in the US. Moreover, the US life styles are the biggest exports of the Americans. I have seen individuals in India, Dubai and Malaysia running from one meeting to the other—while constantly talking on their mobile phones. People of my generation are still resistant to time planners. Every day, I look around my students carrying cell phones that have all their appointments and due dates of papers, tests and exams etc. Some of my colleagues pull a Palm Pilot to check their calendar and stencil an appointment in a few seconds.

Gone are the days of hard diaries. But a funny story is that last month my electronic savvy daughter reverted to hard diary after losing all the data in her Palm organizer due to non-replacement of batteries on time! I am sure that the next generation of Palms will take care of this problem. My fear is of losing the gadget itself, as I have limited my focus only on two things, my wallet and keys!

In the US, the stakes are rising for missing a meeting or an appointment—no matter what your position is. It has a Domino effect. Hence starting a meeting at an Indian Standard time is just out of question. I check my calendar on my office PC at least twice a day as the secretaries in the Dean's office need access to my calendar for appointments with students and scheduling committee meetings. Before leaving the office, I check it for my next day's activities. I don't want to look at it from my home PC just to be able do and think of other things. Having not been a good manager of time, I am learning to say no and not enter every call as an appointment.

I remember some old time Indian friends who used say, "Hey, let us have some **GUPP SHUPP** (means BS-ing) for a little relaxation." Those conversations are now a history. The specter of US Time has changed us! It is amazing to see the falling prices of electronics items—including PCs, and the rising cost of time! Putting it in perspective, during this year's Sunday Super Bowl, the cost of a 30-second commercial is fixed at 2.3 million dollars! The pace at which the events are taking place unless we effectively manage our time, the Time will manage us out!

(Jan 29, 2004)

COMMENTS

What is this life if, full of care, We have no time to stand and stare.
No time to stand beneath the boughs, And stare as long as sheep or cows.
No time to see, when woods we pass, Where squirrels hide their nuts in grass.
No time to see, in broad daylight, Streams full of stars, like skies at night.
No time to turn at Beauty's glance, And watch her feet, how they can dance.
No time to wait till her mouth can, Enrich that smile her eyes began.
A poor life this if, full of care, We have no time to stand and stare.

Dad, Upon reading your article, I began to realize how in this country even life's biggest events are governed by the clock and calendar. For example, as we organize this wedding, I'm finding that it is very difficult to make Mom understand the concept of a timeline. I myself had to learn the importance of organizing my time when I got my job at EF. Forgetting a meeting or an appointment could have costed me my job! Later, when I helped organize a conference of 3,000 educators for Dr. Jane McCarthy, I further realized how important it is that events must be punctually executed.

Now as we begin to send out invitations, I think it's essential that all invitations be sent out together at the same time. Can you imagine how tempers would flare if one guest happened to receive an invitation a few days before another?! The difference between a good social event and a bad one is all about organization and keeping to the schedule. While others make fun of America's obsession with time, I think it is what makes this country tick so perfectly! Good writing. **Annie**

It has been said that time is like money— the less we have of it to spare, the further we make it go! That is the essence of time management in a society with so much money . . . and so little time. **Avnish**

A PARADOX IN COMMUNICATION

Public speaking is the second biggest fear amongst people. The first, of course, is the fear of death. In order to develop speaking skills, I took a course, but it only scratched the surface. Five years ago, I decided to join a toastmasters club. **Communication has two parts: listening and speaking**.

In a club meeting, it takes only three seconds to walk from a seat to the lectern. Often, I forget the opening lines in these three seconds. On returning to the seat, I would wonder, as to how could I forget it? With stage practice, my overall anxiety is getting less, but a 'sudden loss of memory' at the lectern does recur in different scenarios. Fortunately, it does not freeze me up.

There seem to be two analyses. One, in anticipation of my name being called on the stage, a pounding of the heart and a rush of adrenalin may be contributing to a sudden 'rewiring' of brain cells. It may be like a surge of high voltage that trips one circuit, and then the current may go over to the other. That is why I don't end up saying what I want to say, but say what I did not plan on saying.

The other angle is as soon as I am in front of the audience, the very process of the audience looking at me may bring a sudden change in my neurons. **After all, any process of observation is a shower of photons!** It is a fact that cheering or booing from an audience does affect the performance of the players and entertainers, in particular. The sightless persons are not affected in the same measure.

Being the current President of TNT Toastmasters Club, the initial and final segments of the meeting fall into my duties. At the end, there are only 3-4 items left—not taking more than 3-5 minutes. Last Monday, I forgot to announce the winners of the day for the third time in a row! That is what I call a Paradox in Public Speaking.

(Feb 26, 2004)

WHEN WALKING REVEALS

Sometimes, I really wonder at the convergence of different strands of thoughts at one point. A month ago, I indicated in my bio, required for a toastmasters' speech contest that one of my hobbies was Thinking. Last Saturday, I was kind of caught off guard when the presiding toastmaster asked, "Satish, from your bio I am curious about your hobby of **Thinking**. Tell us about it." I did not want to digress by saying that a university professorship means being paid to Think, particularly, when it comes to research in one's field. However, I narrated an incident that had taken place on the same Saturday morning.

It was a beautiful day and after a two-hour walk, I was back in my neighborhood. On noticing two Afro-American women hesitatingly standing in a driveway, I greeted them. One of them asked, "Do you live here?" "Yes," said I, and noted they had some literature in their hands. "Would you like to have this Bible Literature?" "No, I am already familiar with it."

It is not right to politely accept even advertising material and then trash it. As I continued my walk, one of them remarked, "**Enjoy your walk**." These words drove right into my heart. Yes, I do enjoy walking. Turning around, smilingly I said, "**If you enjoy your walk, then it becomes a Bible**." They were obviously non-pulsed. One of them said, "What!" And, I clearly repeated, "If you enjoy your walk, then it is a Bible" Leaving them bewildered and feeling a bit amused at my observation, I resumed my walking.

A state of joy in walking is reached, when the mundane chores are flushed out in an early segment of the walk. Gradually, walking becomes nearly meditative. **You get new ideas and resolve lingering conflicts**. The great ideas in all the scriptures are the results of meditative states of mind, when the body is either sitting still or in walking mode. Any written form of scripture comes much later.

Isn't it tragic that millions of people in history have been killed over sacrileges of holy books of one community or the other? In history, frequent riots and fights take place over sacrileges against the Quran of the Muslims and Guru Granth Sahib of the Sikhs. The universal wisdom crystallizes in the minds the seers before its book form is turned out. The open sky and air are permeated with wisdom, and await for a ripened mind to draw it from the environment.

Incidentally, I did finish this piece right after my walk today. In the US, jaywalking, in some public areas after certain hours, is prohibitive. Essentially, that is what the Indians believe in: that don't be at a wrong place at a wrong time!

(March 27, 2004/Feb, 2012)

COMMENTS

1. Thinking is one of my delights. **Dutchie**

2. It was a wonderful thing. If you enjoy your walk it becomes a Bible. Life cannot be enjoyed unless one is honest to a great degree and one loves people, and one creates. If you are doing it already, you don't need Bible and for that matter . . . . any philosophy . . . . But I am very pleased indeed that YOUR JAY WALKING (or did you mean to say JOY WALKING) is a BIBLE. I hope many more people will be ABLE TO SAY IT. Good DAY. **Subhash Sood**

3. If walking brings you peace of mind then it is Bible for you. After all the whole purpose of religion and spirituality is peace of mind and tranquility. **Rahul**

4. Good thinking!! I believe in this era we want efficiency everywhere. We do not want to waste time; we want to accomplish more in short time. However, as you said, walking or simply sitting may not necessarily a waste of time. I get my best ideas in the middle of the night when I am quietly lying down. During the waking hours I am so busy doing things that I cannot resolve anything. I do enjoy walking and yes, it is therapeutic. Best wishes, **Prafulla**

PETS EXTEND COMMUNICATION

In conversations with white Americans, in particular, besides weather and sports, the next popular topic is pets. The way they describe stories of their pets is deep. On telling them that my pets have always lived in freedom and out of the house, I get puzzled looks. Pets bring out a communication skill of a different order. I tell my wife that if the Hindus claim to communicate with their gods enshrined in idols, then communicating with pets is easier? **Enlightenment is Communication with everything in the Universe.**

For some time, I have been enjoying the company of pigeons in the morning. As soon as I open the patio door, I hear fluttering of their wings and watch them swooping down on me. Perched on the rooftop, they just wait for me to come out. Usually, I have some left over bread and rice for them. In case, my hands are empty; they would just circle around me telling—it is OK. Once in a while, I carry my morning cup of tea and sip it sitting under a fig tree. Drinking tea being meditative, I signal them to wait till I finish tea.

This routine is simple. As I spread the crumbs on a small table 5-6 pigeons fly on it and start pecking. Pigeons never fly away with crumbs in their peeks. They repeatedly strike the food in such a manner that if the piece is large, then they chip away a miniscule; eat it leaving the bigger portion for the next shot, and so on till all is gone in their stomach. Once in a while, a small sparrow would stealthily enter the scene, grab a big crumb and fly away. Pigeons never wonder, or chase the sparrow to snatch the food.

The group behavior of pigeons, on food, is similar to humans. As long as I am dropping the crumbs on the table they scurry after food without any fight. Once I am done and crumbs getting fewer, pushing and shoving begin. Usually, the strongest pigeon remains after the rest are pushed off the table one by one. It is a sight to see this bully feasting on the minute particles. Its tiny red and round eyes meet mine, as if seeking my approval.

While being fed, they would let me pet and finger through their feathers. The power it takes to fly without a run generates so much body heat that it can be felt through the feathers. The noteworthy fact is a strong air draft caused by only one pigeon, as it flies off the table. I tried to imagine a plane that would flutter its wings for flying without a run. The wings will just break off the body. A 747 plane taking off without a run may knock down every structure within 100 yards by its powerful turbulences.

If I am gone for a few days, the pigeons exhibit every temper. Pigeons and humans are creatures of habit. On return, I try to make it up with an extra feed. Once, a cat, on getting scent of the pigeons, was seen lying in ambush. She too being a pet, I loudly warned her to go and prey elsewhere. I know pigeons are cat's favorite meals, but my guts are not strong enough to let the cat pounce on one in my presence. The pigeons trust me for some food and security. **Isn't that a bottom line in any relationship?**

(Sep 15, 2004/Mar, 12)

I LOVE BABY TALK

Ever since my grandson, Amaru (amongst his infinitely many names) began responding to sounds, I have been phoning him every day. It is around the age of 8-10 weeks that an infant shows signs of voice recognition. **It is not that the infants do not hear before this age, but we adults simply are not tuned to understand them!** According to the modern pre-natal researches, a fetus after 3-4 months starts reacting to certain external stimuli. In the Hindu epic, Mahabharata, Abhimanyu learnt specific battlefield strategies while still in his mother's womb. His father Arjun, a great warrior, used to tell militaristic stories to his wife during pregnancy.

This is not the first time that I am doing it. I enjoy infants smiling when they are baby talked, and a little bit 'roughed' up. It may sound meaningless to adults and even jarring to some. However, you must do whatever gives a mutual pleasure. My children and two other grandchildren grew up on it, and so did my two siblings, who are 15-17 years younger than me.

With Amaru the situation is very different. He lives 500 miles away. During the last ten months, I have seen him only thrice. The surprise feature of my gibberish talk is that I speak it in Punjabi! No one speaks in Punjabi at home—including my son and daughter-in-law. Being the first paternal grandson, I have also turned it into an experiment with an hypothesis that Amaru will eventually develop an affinity for Punjabi language.

My son and daughter-in-law have been supportive to my hypothesis. Father being a computational mathematician and mother a physician, Amaru has an abundance of Einstein, Bach and Beethoven in audio tapes to supposedly stimulate his intellectual growth. However, for the first couple of years, physical growth is the foundation for mental development too.

Sometimes, my wife is puzzled and feels embarrassed at my talking to Amaru in public. On the contrary, I am surprised at the parents and relatives who don't indulge in it. Everyone has heard the stories of Ram Krishen Paramhans (1834-1886) speaking with his deity Ma (Mother) symbolized in the idol. During moments of indecision, he used to converse standing in front of her idol, as one does with a person. The Hindus believe that the idols are no longer mere clay, wood, or stone, but their faith infuse life into them. My one brother-in-law daily speaks to his deities in a monologue for

15-20 minutes standing in front of a mini temple set up inside a cupboard of his bedroom.

I believe that the so-called non-living matter is living too, but in a state that one needs the surcharged *yogic* eyes and ears of a Ram Krishen to see and hear it. **However, this experience is highly individualistic.** The idol worship (***MOORTI POOJA***) becomes a societal problem when generalized to the non-Ram Krishen masses. The idols did not protect even the lives of Hindu priests, when the marauding Arabs started smashing them in the 10th century.

Well, if once in a while, some results are positive with the idols, then my experiment with Amaru is on a far solid footing. The periodic repetition of certain word sounds would register on his mind like it does on a CD. It is all scientific. Six weeks ago, I attended a lecture on language learning. **I was delighted to hear when the speaker informed that an infant can learn 40-45 new words per day**! It is child's remarkable ability to imitate in speaking that a language comes easy for which the adults struggle.

My son and daughter-in-law often tell me how Amaru suddenly stops his activity at hand the moment he hears my voice on the phone. He wants to grab the phone and put it in his mouth! For an infant, mouth is the only receptor for all his sensory inputs. I repeat that no English word is spoken. Try it, if you are fortunate to have this blessing. Be a baby first!

(Nov 14, 2004/March, 2012)

COMMENTS

1. Nice article; I'm sure Arman especially will enjoy reading it in a few years! Of course, *non-verbal* communication with others also plays a key role in a child's development . . . as the attached photo attests! — **Avnish**

2. Made for each other. Grandfather and grandson. Both of them orators. But why did you start with Punjabi and not Hindi? I thought Hindi was your mother tongue. **Rahul**

I wrote: While growing up in Punjab, we all brothers and sister spoke in Hindi with each other in home and outside, but in Punjabi with others. Besides, Punjabi language has a lot of robust phrases that come easily in baby talking too. More variety!

3. Most of us have similar experiences, but have not given due thought and recognition to the natural instinct which comes from the day one is born. You have tried to give some sort of 'truth' an almost correct phenomenon in human life based on your experiences in general and your talking in Punjabi with Amaru. The universal message of this is 'do not undermine a kid's capacity to understand and respond. **NIGAM**

4. The reflection about your grandson was fascinating. **Gayathri**

5. Dear Satish Bhai, Namaste: Delighted to know about ur personal intimate verbal interactive experiences with dear Amaru. The most fascinating aspect is, that u had been striking the right interactive chord with various age groups, with the likes of Esther etc But here u have traveled deeper into human sensorial finesse. Yes, children do have cognitive power of voice recognition, correlation of repetitive words or phrases, as early as the last trimester of the pregnancy. They start responding to the extent their expressive faculties have developed. Until articulative facilities have developed, they struggle to do it with other body languages. My wife does a lot of talks with her grand children. Her vibes get astonishing response in grunts, giggles and monosyllabic efforts. I request u to keep me informed about ur Punjabi language feed to the g/ children. It will b an interesting experiment. **Ravi**

ON A PROTOCOL OF DYING

"I can't study at all because my 20-year old close friend and neighbor of 6-7 years died this morning. Since last Friday, he was in a trauma center due to a motorbike accident. My biggest regret is that I did not go to see him in the hospital." That is a gist of what my student told me last Monday. It was around noon, and I told him to be with his friend's family. It would lessen the feelings of guilt. I also suggested him not to miss classes, and make no efforts to concentrate too much either. While consoling, I said, since the prayers have healing powers, your thinking of your friend must have sent him a telepathic message. Finally, I brought him in contact with my pastor friend for spiritual counseling.

A similar incident took place just last week. The grandfather of a close acquaintance was in his last stages of life. He was in a comma when the word reached. He decided not to go and see him. He presumed it was useless since the grandfather won't be able to see and talk to him anyways.

These incidents stirred a few personal memories on death and dying. My maternal grandfather took his last breath with full consciousness. It happened 45 years ago in Bathinda (BTI), while I was gone for my master's in Chandigarh. I did not go to attend his funeral. Suddenly, my mind completely went off the studies. I really panicked about my mind. Fortunately, I discussed it with my late teacher and distinguished mathematician, HR Gupta. Immediately, he instructed me to leave for BTI. Normalcy came back after a couple of days! By listening to his last moments funeral from my mother, uncle and brothers, a quick closure came upon this chapter of life. I may add, that his influence during the formative years of my life continues to this day.

The *Tibetan Book of the Dead* is a classic on the art and science of dying moments and the transference of soul to the other plane. It is medically established that out of the five senses, eyes are the first one to stop its business of seeing, and then comes taste, smell, and touch at certain points of the body. Sense of hearing is the last one to say 'good bye'. That is why in every religion and creed, either some recitation of certain passages of scriptures, or playing of favorite musical tunes near the departing one, is very common.

My gut feelings are that I won't linger on a deathbed. My checkout from Planet Earth will be swifter than that of my father, mother, and maternal grandfather. Nevertheless, if I do go in a comma, then don't stay away. Just once, come to my side and privately whisper into my ears whatever comes out from your head and heart—while touching my palm. Afterwards, go back to your routines. It will make my passage to the 'other world' easier—also a quick closure for all my near and dear ones. On the contrary, Bhishma Peetamah, in the Hindu epic, *Mahabharata,* says that withdrawal of the life force from the body is as painful as the stings of a thousand scorpions on the body. I would defy it!

(March 10, 2005/March, 2012)

COMMENTS

1. Dear Satish; I hereby send my Supreme Postulate that you may get the type of Death you wish to have, as described by you in your letter. Death can be under some control. Life has to do with a Goal, a purpose, a destination. And when one destination is achieved, another must be kept ready. Otherwise Yamraj will knock the door. I have no plans or wish or Postulate to die during next couple or three decades. And I plan to remain healthy and up and about like other active people. **Subhash Sood** (Died in April 2007—only two years later from a massive stroke!)

2. This one is good, but very short. There could have been another perspective here. My 2 bits worth. I have had a friend die too and that was a very bad thing for me. He had an accident and we visited almost every day. But he died in the 2 days I didn't visit and that makes me sad. I should have been able to say good bye. This was 12 years ago and I still remember the day he died—April 10. I didn't need any counseling or anything and I am not religious, but I am spiritual—so I guess I coped that way. My maternal grandparents died when I was old enough to understand and know about death, but they didn't linger and they lived long lives. In my case, I did attend their funerals and that did give some sense of closure.

This is an interesting perspective—because I think the Tibetan book of the dead tries to explain something that no one has been able to explain at any stage. Maybe there is no other plane at all; maybe we are just glorified animals with all our sense of self-awareness and our tampering with the eco system and our inventions. Maybe the search for god will yield nothing. **Aniruddha**

3. Laai Hayaat to aaye qaza le chali chaley
   Apni Khushi se na aaye na apni khushi chaley
   Kam hongey is bisaat par hum aisey bad qumaar
   Jo chaal hum chaley woh nihayat buri chaley
   Behtar to hai yehi ke na duniya se dil lagey
   Par kya karein jo kaam na be dil-lagi chaley
   Duniya ne kis ka raah-e-fanaa mein diya hai saath tum bhi chaley chalo
   yunhi jab tak chali chaley
   Jaatey Hawaa-e-shauq mein hain is chaman se Zauq
   Apni balaa se Baad-e-Saba ab kabhi chaley

(Its English Translation)
The life brought me so I came; the death takes me away so I go
Neither I came on my own nor I go with my will
There may be a few gamblers as bad as I am
Whatever move I made it proved to be very bad
It's better that one should not get hooked to the charms of the world
However, what one can do when nothing can be accomplished without getting involved
Who's come to the rescue of someone who's about to leave this world!
You too keep moving till you can move on
O Zauq! I'm leaving this garden with a pinning for fresh air
Why should I care now whether zephyr blows or not! **Rahul**

4. After the demise of my grandson Nitin, I got broke and am not able to come up with normal life even today. My greatest regret is that I could not see him in the hospital where he remained for nine days. Just when we were going to the hospital, message of his death came. I got worst shock of my life. Nitin was the greatest help to me and was planning his post-secondary work at Delhi University till he gets into the USA. Among my siblings he was the most appreciating and helpful of my work, thinking and value system. My first remark was that "MEREY DONO HATH KAT GAI'. THANKS FOR E-MAIL REFLECTIONS. **NIGAM**

5. I'm so touched by the honesty and deep feelings in this essay. Your messages of compassion and understandings of human relationships and the truth are so logical and necessary for peace in life. I am grateful. See you in the morning for an adventure. **Dutchie**

PERSONAL COMMENTS

I MISS WEEDS!

"I gave $20 to the girls to take all the weeds out of the front yard." declared my wife yesterday, as I walked into the house. I cringed a little, but did not say a word. I liked those weeds. During springtime, they burst out of the soil—showing yellow flowers only along the edges of sidewalks. Our front yard landscape is environmentally friendly with cacti, rocks and boulders. While going in and out of the house, I pluck a few flowers along with their tiny stems and chew them. They taste pungent like radish. It has not hurt me over the years. I am certain they may have built my immune system. Today, they were all gone!

Americans are dead against the weeds. Visit a nursery and one can find every tool needed to take a weed out no matter the nook and corner it grows from. Then, there are sprays and chemical weed killers. A related popular story, from the life of Chanakya, the chief counselor of the Mauryan Empire (ca 300 BC), comes to my mind. While walking bare foot near his abode, he stepped on a thorny ground cover. Even after digging its roots out, he poured sour buttermilk in the root system to ensure that it never grows there again. That was a Hindu mindset for not forgetting and forgiving the enemy. Centuries later, Prithviraj Chauhan ignored this lesson. He repeatedly defeated his enemy, but never killed him. Finally, when he lost, it changed the history of the Hindus for the next 1000 years!

In old brick houses of India, parasite plants shoot out of the flying seeds stuck in the crevices. One of the commonly seen plants is *PEEPAL* that some Hindus even worship it. In small towns, trunks of *PEEPAL* trees have red and yellow marks and (***KALAWA***) sacred thread wrapped around them. Consequently, most Hindus don't extract *PEEPAL* saplings sticking out of the walls, ledges and edges of the roofs! During our 1980-82 stay in India, I enjoyed re-potting and transforming them into **BONSAI *PEEPAL*** trees.

My thoughts on weeds extend the whole panorama of life. Two years ago, my Department Head, a Haitian-American had a hell of time from his white neighbors. He was, perhaps, a human weed for them! His education, status and earnings did not matter to his neighbors. Being a history buff, I am sure, **the Native Americans (mistakenly called Indians from India) did not treat the first white settlers as weeds in America!**

I see a justification, if in a pampered grassy lawn, green clovers spring up. Yes, some golf courses in Las Vegas are given a care befitting queens. We like symmetry and patterns to a large extent. For this reason little weeds are snuffed out of existence in no time! Due to hot, dry and little precipitation, nothing grows in Las Vegas, unless some rich fertile top soil is brought and irrigated with sprinklers. I tell my wife that the so-called weed will die out as they are born, so why to abort them? I am very certain of usefulness of their brief span of life. For me, the weeds defy a dichotomy between living and non-living. Weed, or not a weed, is a real question!

(Mar 13, 2005/Mar, 2012)

COMMENTS

1. **A weed is a plant whose virtues are yet to be discovered.**

It is a story that once at the end of education a student of Ayurveda went to his Guru and ceremoniously asked for blessings. The guru said," You have been with me for a number of years and now the time has come when you are equal to me in terms of knowledge. But before the final parting I want to test your capability and receive my gurudakshinaa as well. So, please bring me a plant which has no medicinal value. If you are able to bring one, it will satisfy me on both the counts." The student went on and on searching for such a plant. After six months of frantic search he came back empty handed and admitted that he could find none. The guru was elated and said," you have completed your education now. Go away and afar and work to the benefit of man and his kind" **Raman**

I wrote: Simply beautiful!

Raman: Sir, I liked your essay on weeds. Our flat in Delhi is on the top floor, so we have good access to the rooftop where we have about forty planters in which we have planted various plants like, Tulsi, Maura, dhania, pudina, gulab, etc. etc. but I have purposely left about 10 planters without any sowing. I filled them with soil and watered them regularly. I just wanted the nature to intervene. Lo and behold, in no time they were full of different kinds of plants. Some of them were totally unknown to me. They are beautiful and mysterious. They are like guests in my little garden.

2. Barring some exceptions most who migrate are weeds for their native land and then they become weed for population in their host country. A middle aged Kashmiri refugee woman (weed for Muslims of Kashmir just like Jews were weeds for Hitler) came into my front yard and sought permission to remove certain weeds, which were in fact medicinal plants Weed or not weed depends upon the survival needs of the species who is dominating, which happens to be Man on the planet. White man in America (African American are weeds and Indians from Bharat are semi weeds.) **Subhash**

3. Weeds are flowers too, once you get to know them. **Rahul**

4. Dear Sh Bhatnagar, I continue to read with deep interest your articles. Some of the articles really show the keen observations by you. Some

social and spiritual articles have been enjoyable as well as informative. Recent articles, I miss weeds, On a protocol of dying, Cross road of Indian community were quite informative and enjoyable. **Hardev**

5. Interesting article—I liked it immensely. What is a weed? Is it something that does not conform to our viewpoint/expectations? If it is something that does not conform to our viewpoint/expectations and that is the only reason we terminate it. Then doesn't it go a long way to describe us as a human society? Maybe that is a reason about discrimination—we think of all those who do not fall in a set pattern as weeds. Another thought . . . What is a weed? Isn't it an underdog, a survivor perhaps? It grows where nobody wants it to grow. Nobody expects it survive with all the weed killers etc—but it survives and thrives. Yet nobody likes it. We say, we always root for the underdog—but do we? Or do we just root for underdogs that conform to expected patterns and not weeds. **Vicky—**

WHEN YOU BECOME SPEECHLESS

Major US universities are both microcosm and macrocosm of the entire society. Over 27,000 students walk on UNLV's 325-acre campus. While strolling out today, I noticed a young girl sitting on a brick hedge of a planting area. I had almost passed by her that suddenly my eyes, following her bare shoulder, stopped at her left upper arm ending in a stub! Immediately, I retraced my steps back to her.

She was sitting composed and I discovered that her both arms were missing! "How did you lose them—was there some accident?" For a moment, I thought of a Las Vegas poster girl, Mary, who 20 years ago was abducted and her both hands were hacked away. "I was born like this!" She replied. I mumbled and felt speechless. In the US, most handicapped persons want to be treated with dignity and they are not hesitant to talk about their infirmities.

From her features, she looked like from Indian subcontinent. "What are you studying for a major?" I was curious. "Computer graphics—I have changed it from architecture." She replied. Bewildered that she has no hand, or prosthetics, I said, "How do you use computers?" Promptly, she indicated by moving her right foot. Then I talked about an organization of foot and mouth artists of USA, who paint by holding the brushes in mouths or toes.

While indirectly assuring her by telling about my being a professor, I asked her name. The way she pronounced, it sounded strange. She then spelled it out as Shanthi Scanner. "Oh, Shanti! It is an Indian name; that means peace." She nodded. It was obvious that she was at peace with her conditions. "But your last name is not typically Indian," I said. "It is American, I was adopted," she added. That unleashed a stream of thoughts in my minds.

"You are an inspiration!" I told her. Suddenly, she said, "Here is my ride." She got up, adjusted her backpack with a shrug and straight she walked. I remained there; my eyes were still fixed on her. With a little bent, she opened the car door, jerked her backpack off into the back seat. Then, she got into the passenger seat and closed the door with her right toe.

The nameless faces of hundreds of blind, maimed, crippled beggar kids in India crowded my mind. This girl could have been one of them. Generally, the Hindus are known to dump such children out on the streets and orphanages for weird religious beliefs—including bad omens. But the magnanimity of one American couple yanked Shanthi out of that hell and brought her in an environment, where she shall be what she wants to be.

Long live the spirit of America! **The greatness of a nation is measured by the greatness achieved by the greatest number of its ordinary people**.

(May 03, 2005/Mar, 2012)

COMMENTS

1. This is so heavy. If only every high school student could interview Shanti in depth as you did on the campus walk. That would be one wish for me. I'd be shaken and touched to my depths if I had been with you to listen to her story. Her parents are saints here on earth. **Dutchie**

2. My dear Bhatnagar Sahib, Namaskar. This one left me speechless as well. My God what candid thought and reflection. One thing seems for sure now that you must have decided never to come back and live in India for good. **Jagjeet**

3. It is our greatest misfortune that the entire Indian sub-continent (especially the Hindu society) dumps handicaps and helpless (widows) to streets/Varanasi/Mathura on the plea of misfortune for the entire family if such a member lives with them. Arya Samaj has done a lot to bring an end to such practices, of course with limited success only. We should feel ashamed for such practices, and fears; they are inhuman by ALL STANDARDS. **NIGAM**

4. So you are saying in India only Hindus dump their children who are not physically complete and people of other religions do not. Only Americans adopt these children and no other nation does it. Majority of Americans do that. No American does such heinous acts like Hindus do. Correct? I am speechless with your assumptions. Research does not seem to be your asset when your write these articles. So I am not surprised with the result. If your idea to write Reflections is bash Hindus then you are doing pretty well and "continue with it". May God bless you. **Rahul**

I wrote: Isn't it almost proverbial that there is no Sikh beggar? Still one can find a beggar who is a Sikh. Take Christians now. One convoluted Hindu belief is that beggars nurture pity in the hearts!

Rahul: So you have not been to Amritsar. You can see Sikh beggars by dozens. What about Muslim beggars you conveniently by passed them. In Islam giving alms (Zakat) is a must. Go to Goa and you will find Christian beggars. When you see panhandlers in this country you must be thinking these unfortunate people are Hindus. Then by your thinking there should be no beggars outside India or Nepal. **That is why I say you do not research before you write.** Any way your article was about **only** Hindus throwing away their deformed, inauspicious babies and **only** magnanimous American Christians taking them with open arms into their homes. Now how more convoluted in thinking can one get?

I wrote: I heard the stories of Hindu beggars in the garbs of Sikh, Christians and Muslims in popular places. Zakat is not to encourage beggary but to minimize it. Panhandlers are not beggars. They are socialists who can catch your collars and take money out of the pockets!

Rahul: beggars in all Muslim and Christian countries are Hindus. You have quite a bit of imagination. So these Hindus got businesses visa to do beg there. Ha Ha Ha. Zakat is to discourage beggary that is a new one too. Khairat is another Islamic tradition encouraged by Allah. But then per you people receiving Khairat are Hindu's in Muslim grab.

I think Panhandlers are the Capitalists who lost money in stock market but by force of habit have not given up habit of fleecing general public. But per you they are Hindus.

This reminds of some Hindus I knew in Punjab who were too ashamed to be Hindus but were also too scared to convert.

I wrote: Sometimes I really think as if I wrote your comments 20 years ago! You sure keep me on my toes. Don't forget they are Reflections; not essays, or sociol-psychological or historical articles. Yes, I do have an uncanny ability to make or suggest connections between two very diverse platforms whether in my math classes or in these writings. Thanks again.

Rahul: Without true facts and research even the reflections lose their luster. In muddled waters one cannot see anything. Any ways keep up the good work.

I wrote: Here is a Mantra, a mathematical theorem, or call it a Quantum Theory of Identification: It is all Maya. There are no absolute facts; it is always yours vs. mine. Numbers lie as it depends upon who do they belong to. History is a perpetuation of lies, or call them non-facts. Yet, the paradox is that so much including life and death rest on them! Thanks for helping me bring these nuggets out!

Rahul: *hum ko maloom hai jannat ki haqiqat lekin dil ke Khush rakhane ko 'Ghalib' ye Khayaal achcha hai*

However, I never thought your idea of writing "My Reflections" was to dispel Maya. However a good Researcher does not shy away from things which were not part of the hypothesis. Research is search for truth be it Maya.

5. Satish, The story of the armless girl brought tears to my eyes. She truly is an inspiration and you have given her a chance to inspire many more people by writing about her! Thank you for sharing! **Karla Rehm**

IT IS ALL IN THE ROOTS

This morning, I was walking on a sidewalk lined with tall trees in front of the houses that must be 30 years old. It is easy to guess the age from the growth of trees and exteriors of the houses. **The cement sidewalk was wavy, but not from California earthquake**! At some spots, depending on the size of a tree, the cement pavement was lifted up right at the middle to a height of nearly 9"! At others, the slabs were broken in two or three places. It is the cumulative effect of the perpetual forces underneath! The roots were doing the damage. The trees, planted in the center of the front lawns, had raised the ground into the form of a mound nearly two-foot high! It is the silent power of the tiny roots that grow stronger over the years.

My thoughts switched to the world of human beings. Can the spirit of man be crushed forever? There have been men—like Veer Savarkar (India) and Nelson Mandela (South Africa), who were tortured in the prisons for over 20 years. Their spirits could not be broken. Once they were freed, they made new histories. On the other hand, the British colonizers in Australia, New Zealand, Canada and USA broke the will of the indigenous people. It happened in some African countries too. The Hindu survived 1000 years of numerous foreign subjugations in India itself. Though, their quality of life remains questionable.

The previous house we lived had Mulberry trees in the backyard and Ashwood's in front. The developers had them planted. After ten years, the root system lifted and broke a huge chunk of the corner of the neighbor's driveway. That alerted me. With a pickaxe, I carefully dug out to the depth of the cement slab along its edges and pulled out nearly 100' of chunky roots— some 2" thick in diameter! It must have saved the foundation of my house. Once, when our kitchen sink was clogged, it was discovered that invisible fine roots of a tree in the front yard had entered the PVS pipe at the joints!

The individual Muslim terrorists are like the invisible roots. The 9/11 Attack did not happen overnight. They have infiltrated the free democratic societies and are working with sleeper cells in these countries. Does it mean that any weak group will eventually become strong enough to overthrow an entrenched power? The answer is yes and no. In Aug 1945, the US brought the WW II to an end, when the Japanese continued to wage war on the Eastern front after the surrender of Germany in May, 1945. Two nuclear bombs broke the fighting will of the Japanese forever. A new Japan was born—democratic and open. If the US Government had the same mind set, as it was in the 1940s, then on Oct 10, 2001, it would have dropped one nuclear bomb on Afghanistan. It would have broken the will of Al Qaida. As a corollary, there would have been no Iraqi operation.

(Aug 19, 2005/LA)

COMMENTS

1. Who do you think is responsible for nurturing these (trees) extremists? There masters or gardeners or growers were the politicians from these "democratic western society." They fed and propagated and nurtured them to meet their own ends. They are like Frankenstein's monster which is not in control of its master. As about Iraqi insurgency Bush administration is singularly responsible for it. This is another monster created by Bush which will take a generation to control. Big leaders do not make mistakes they make blunders. These are unfortunate times for world when our leaders are short sighted. **Rahul**

I wrote: No need to pin the blame on any one. I took out 100' root system is the way to take these sleepers out! Yes, big leaders pay heavy price even for small mistakes—like Clinton.

Rahul: Why not to pin the blame on people who are at fault? Clinton was the best thing which happened to USA since Apple pie but as day is followed by night so Clinton was followed by minion like our present President. But despair not. You think you took all the roots with those 100 roots then think again or better dig again.

I wrote: We love the shade and fruits of trees too. You are right taking roots out is not one time, but once in ten years is good enough.

Rahul: Just keep one thing in mind we too are transplanted non-Christian non-Anglo trees in this country and our roots (Hinduism, Sikhism and new age) could also damage their (Christian) foundations. So think twice about your nuke options. If you think you are safe then remember that Japanese and Germans during WW 11 were put in camps.
I wrote: Come on Rahul! The Hindu roots are innocuous, as their history in 65 countries of the last 100 years means anything. They don't own their Hindustan!! When would you wake up?

Rahul: I think you are in a deep slumber by thinking that you are safe from Christian Conservatives in this country. These people like Pat Robertson see no difference between brown-skinned heathens.

I wrote: Let us say for the argument's sake, Hindus have to choose between Christian Conservatives (Very few) and Islamic Fundamentalists (Very many), then where do you align?

Rahul: Neither! It is a choice between **Rock and a Hard Place**. Do you know what havoc these Christian Conservatives are causing in North Eastern India? Christian Conservatives now control the most powerful country in the world and their actions are more subtle and damaging then radical Muslims.

I wrote: That is the story of a typical Hindu; not to stand up and align boldly! Question is now and here in the US. If you are that afraid of CC while living in USA, then ask the Hindus and Sikhs living/leaving Pakistan/Afghanistan/Kashmir, or in any Muslim country.

Rahul: So, you are atypical Hindu. Standing up for oneself does not mean that one advocates nuking others. Living in this country, we have to unite against CC and not support their puppet which foolishly some of my fellow Hindus did.

A SYMPATHY CHECK-UP

A display of even genuine sympathy by some sympathizers can be annoying to some sympathizees. With the exception of attention hungry individuals, it is not often welcomed after age 60 when the emotional arteries begin to harden up. Of course, a child, in its innocence, is always buoyed up with any attention. The adults have mixed reactions.

Recently, our iron lady neighbor was admitted in a hospital and wanted no visitors including her friends. Her husband was indirectly informed. She was 'upset' when her Indian friend still went to the hospital to 'lift her spirits'. Some individuals never want to be seen down in body or spirits. In this regards, my wife and I belong to different camps.

While growing up in India, we were drilled that one should join in others' moments of sorrow and celebration. **It requires setting aside a hell of jealousy in being happy in the happiness of others!** Grief is divided when shared (only with near and dear ones). I believed and practiced it for many years.

However, once 18 years ago, we went to see an ex-friend admitted in a hospital. Later on, we were relayed back that why had we visited in the moments of illness, when communications had ceased during normal circumstances. It was a moment of new truth that opened my eyes for future.

These thoughts were triggered today when my wife called about my cousin in India. A few days ago, he had angina pains and is now advised to go for heart surgery. He is like my elder brother, as we grew up together—from teen years to adulthood. Nevertheless, for a number of reasons our relationships have been going downhill for the last 10 years. It hit a bottom when during my last visit to India we did not even meet, or phone each other. I told my wife to call India to get the latest, as tomorrow could be my day.

Four years ago, I had a two-side hernia surgery. For me, it was a period of solitude and introspection. Quiet presence of visitors and a few thoughtful words are fine for me. During recuperation, my younger brother (by 15 years) came to see me. He is the type of a person who refused to attend my daughter's wedding and even stopped his family members too. A few months prior to my surgery, he was walking down the same aisle in a Wal-Mart, and on seeing him, I stopped to say hello. But he continued walking by and ignored my existence! Neither, I missed him during my convalescence, nor did his visit make a difference.

During a sympathy visit, appropriate words may not come out off the cuff. But in the USA, there is an apt wording in a card that captures a specific mental state for a particular occasion, provided one takes time to search for it. A greetings card may not be a substitute for a personal visit, but it guarantees minimum side effects!

(Mar 19, 2006)

COMMENTS

1. Hi Satish: Interesting observations on human emotions!! I enjoyed reading it. Your column today brought my own memories of my father. During the last 10-15 years of his life, he was so open to share his feelings that it created problems for my mother and several other members of our family. He was like an open book and was immune to praise as well as criticisms. He just shared his views truthfully to all and helped everyone who came in contact with him. This included strangers, family members, acquaints, and even animals. All street dogs walked behind him, when he went to the nearby market. This is what you have become. You are so open now, sharing your family secrets, your views on different people around you, etc. In a sense, you are liberated now—a condition for desirelessness. This is a stage of life that leads to *Moksha*. Best wishes, **Alok Kumar**

2. I hate sympathy when I am down. I like help when I am down. For many years now I do not suffer from jea . . . . **Subhash**

3. Hi Satish: Greetings! Your 'reflection' is apropos. Sibling relationships may prove to be tough. **Moorty**

4. Dear Satish, Major correction to your facts. I was not "upset" that Anal visited. I was impressed and surprised and delighted. My preference is that I be left alone when ill. Anal is such a dear, sweet human being that it's impossible to be "upset" with him any time and at anything he does. Love and hugs, **Dutchie,** still pondering.

5. *maan jaaye khuda kare koi dard-e-dil ki dawa kare koi* **Rahul**

6. Dear Professor Chandra, I found your reflection delightfully written, morally uplifting, and informative regarding Indian culture. I can see a market for your writings. Selfishly, I have been looking for a peek into Indian values, as I prepare to read some novels by Indian authors this summer. I'm glad our paths crossed. I should be happy to rough edit a selection of your reflections in preparation for your speaking with publishers. Sincerely, **Carolyn Light Cameron**
Part-Time Instructor Dept. of English, UNLV

FISH AND MY REFLECTIONS

A cliché, 'There is something to learn every day' has become a way of life. It has been a great journey of new vistas. The more I *reflect*, the minuter becomes my observation. It is like fishing. My fishing experience, being unique, is now a metaphor. I had no idea of the directions and outcomes of my writings, when I started it three years ago.

Growing up in Bathinda (BTI), which is located on the edge of India's *Great Thar Desert*, water was very scarce then. The fish were seen in the textbooks only. During the 1940s, electricity was not in the households and ice-making plants did not exist. In BTI heat, the fish used to decompose right in front of the eyes. Amongst many soured items, I have eaten stale fish too. That may be a reason for my relatively strong digestive and immune systems. However, the US living softens everyone. Now I resort to an alcoholic drink with any non-vegetarian item even taking it in BTI.

At 14, I bought my first fishing hook, and turned it into an improvised fishing rod. There was a 100' diameter brick lined water reservoir (called *GOLE DIGGI*) in the center of our part of the city. (During the 1960s, it was filled up and developed into *GOLE DIGGI Shopping Complex.*) I recall the excitement of catching 9"-10" long fish, unhooking and cleaning them. Since most of my friends had never tasted fish in their homes, they would share their catch with me. Naturally, appetite for fish and attraction for catching it waned in a short time.

It has been more than 50 years; I have yet to fish in the US, where fishing is a pastime, sport, therapeutic and even contemplative. My energy now finds outlets into fishing of the ideas and turning them into spinning them into *Reflections*. They are no different from culinary fish delights.

Constantly, I catch new varieties of fish. Suddenly, the net becomes wider. At the end of the day, I haul more fishes that I can process! The ones that catch my eyes are taken in, and the rest are tossed back into the waters. Some show up into the net again perhaps for their redemption from this birth!

The fishing net is getting finer too. The tiny sardines and micro fish that used to slip out of the net now shimmer in front of me. I am no longer restricted to one body of water. I can fish anywhere. At times, the fish come swimming to me. Ultimately, I want to swim with the fish, play with the fish and understand the very origin of their world. Writing Reflections becomes an inward journey. Each one takes me to a new depth and insight.

This **Reflection** is being written up on the laptop while sitting in the middle seat during a flight from Las Vegas to Sacramento. The two guys, on my either side, are no distraction. My journey may help in theirs. I am not squeamish about their reading it, as I write for others. It is not a personal journal. Let them take it away its any bits and pieces.

(May 10, 2006)

COMMENTS

1. Your comparison of catching new ideas with fish is fascinating to me. **Subhash**

2. Thanks for sending this. Excellent food for thought. **A K Kundra**

3. Hi Dad, Great reflection. I like the way you guided the reader from the physical act of fishing the comparative message of fishing for ideas etc. **Alex**

4. Hello Satish, Your use of the fish metaphor is interesting . . . . I liked the second last paragraph about swimming with the fish . . . . a very liberating thought . . . . and poetical. Regards, **Sarojini**

TWO LIGHTNING STRIKES

Within a week, two persons, acquainted for several years, have been reportedly afflicted with Lou Gehrig's disease. Coincidentally, both are professors. One is a friend's wife known since 1965, when I was at Kurukshetra University, India. After putting her husband through his PhD in mathematics and raising two children, she started her PhD in Operations Research, at the age of 40. The other is a UNLV history professor known for over ten years. A recent write-up, on his life, released this news to the entire campus.

The disease technically called as Amyotrophic Lateral Sclerosis (ALS) is commonly known after a legendary baseball player, Lou Gehrig (1903-41). It rapidly affects various limbs due to progressive degeneration of the nerve cells in the brain and spinal cord. This colleague is 47, and only last summer, he felt a common twinge in his forearm. His diagnosis and treatment were early and quick. Yet, in six months, his physical condition has come to a point that he finds it difficult to operate the mouse of his PC. He is the author of 15 books, numerous articles, radio talk show host, and a columnist for a local newspaper.

The friend's wife, though diagnosed a year ago, has gone from medical leave to retirement. She is 67. The disease is strange in the sense that whereas, the degeneration of the limbs and their functions is very quick, the mind is least affected. The most famous case is of British astrophysicist, Stephen Hawking living with this disease for over 40 years. His books and researches, despite his debilitating disease, have made him an international icon. In fact, his recently marrying his young secretary made bigger headlines! Men who can never match his intellect are envious of his scores over women.

The breaking up of such news goes through the entire being like a lightning bolt. It suddenly brings mortality closer and the morbid thoughts of death begin to loom on a mental horizon. Momentarily, it freezes life in its track, or makes it jump off to a new track. As my colleague is quoted, "Each day is now an adventure. I was always one of those people who was going to make the most out of every day—and I still am. **This may kill me, but it will never beat me.**"

Whether one is struck with such a disease or close to such a person, it is a reckoning time to take stock of life and relationships. The fear of living from a life of complete independence to total dependence is very real. One may end up without dignity very quickly. The bottom line remains: nothing is immortal; no person or idea has conquered Time. Yet, we all wish to check out from this Planet in a painless mode.

(May 14, 2006)

COMMENTS

1. Dear Satish, Thank you for your thoughtful articles. This one really touched me. I have a brother who is disabled and I know how difficult it is for him to live a life of dependence. Just recently I was mentioning Stephen Hawking to him to boost his morale! My fond wishes for those struck by disability that they will look to the Great Mind for inspiration! Best Wishes, **Usha**

2. Kabir says: (I do not think you need translation)
   Sadho Ye Murdon Ka Gaon, Peer Mare, Pygambar Mari Hain;
   Mari Hain Zinda Jogi, Raja Mari Hain, Parja Mari Hain,
   Mari Hain Baid Aur Rogi; Chanda Mari Hain, Suraj Mari Hain;
   Mari Hain Dharni Akasa
   Chaudan Bhuvan Ke Chaudhry Mari Hain; In Hun Ki Ka Asa
   Nauhun Mari Hain,
   Dus Hun Mari Hain Mari, Hain Sahaj Athasi Tethis Koti Devata
   Mari Hain Badi Kaal Ki Bazi, Naam Anam Anant Rehat Hai Duja
   Tatva Na Hoi
   Kahet Kabir Suno Bhai Sadho, Bhatak Maro Mat Koi-Rahul

3. International ALS gene search begins BALTIMORE, May 16 (UPI) — U.S. scientists are leading the first international gene search for typical ALS — amyotrophic lateral sclerosis, also known as Lou Gehrig's disease. Although it's the more common form of the disease, sporadic ALS — affecting about 90 percent of those living with the fatal neurodegenerative illness — has been the one less studied, simply because, unlike familial ALS, no genes have been determined involved. This week, however Dr. Bryan Traynor and John Hardy of the Packard Center for ALS Research at Johns Hopkins University are beginning the first in-depth screening for genes that underlie the "spontaneous" illness, which, as all ALS, destroys the motor neurons that enable movement, including breathing. Half of the study focuses on Italian populations. "In the forest of exciting research that's going on in ALS," said Packard Director Jeffrey Rothstein, "this is a tall tree. We've been waiting some time for this one." Traynor said the work will clarify the role of genes in sporadic ALS. He added: "We don't know, for example, if (sporadic) ALS is triggered by a handful of interacting genes or genes plus environment or environment alone. The study aims to clarify that." **Dr H N Bhatnagar**

4. A friend mentioned to me that one can only stay normal if one faces near death situation at least twice in a day. I wish to request you to comments on this. I would not like you to just bypass it. One can only make sense of this world if one considers that everyone else is a part of us. This is a fact for me. Everyone living, I am just reminding you, must die quickly or slowly. If some person believes that he is special in some way very different from others he is going to be made equal to others very soon by DEATH. I do not know what your views are, but we do not check out of this planet after death. We remain here or in some cases we leave this planet. You must be thinking that there is no memory. More of it later if the subject does not disinterest you. **Subhash**

5. Bhatnagar Sahib: We had colleague in the early 90's. He had just turned 64 and applied for retirement at the end of the year. He found out in the beginning of the academic year that he had the Lou Gehrig's disease. He withdrew his retirement application and applied for sick leave. He often came by to the department. We could see the rapid deterioration in his muscles. By May next year, his lungs were not strong enough anymore to breathe and died. His wife, otherwise healthy could not bear the loss and passed away within the next six months.

Talking of sad things, another colleague also reaching about 63 decided to take a sabbatical to spend the time in his native Finland. He had heart attack within a week of his arrival there. His wife worked for the registrar's office. She did not feel good on hearing the news of her husband's death and drove to the local hospital to be checked in. She died the same night. Their memorials were held together. Their only son, a ski bum who lived in Colorado doing odd jobs so he could stay near ski resorts and ski, suddenly came up with close to a million dollar inheritance. He blew it in a couple of years and started drifting around again. Life!!! **Ved P. Sharma**

6. Hello Uncle, Thanks for continuing to share your thoughts with us. This reflection of yours definitely hit home for us and I thought of forwarding it to mom as well. We hope you are doing well. With regards, **Charu**

01/10/08 Dinesh died on Jan 03; had spoken with her on Dec 30 at 11 AM. She was 69. In June, 2007, I drove from Detroit to Warren, Ohio and spent a few hours with her and found her at peace with her conditions.

PERSONAL COMMENTS

LIFE IN MY BACKYARD

Sitting on a bench set under a pomegranate tree, I was in a meditative frame over my morning tea. The tea was already finished, but I was gazing blank at the patio cement. One of my morning routines is to feed the pigeons. Today, it was a bread roll that had a green spot of a fungus. In the expiration date driven US culture, most people would be scared to eat it, though it has some medicinal value, since most vaccines are cultured out of fungi.

Besides my 'faithful' pigeons, there are moody sparrows; a colony of tiny brown ants and a few red ants that have found homes in the cracks of the cement. They all irritate my wife. It is pleasing as the pigeons descend down from the rooftops of the houses, as soon as, I come out in the backyard. After a few years of feeding, they have become very friendly that they feed off my hands and perch over my stretched legs. Such a trusting nature can be costly in life. It is the Hindu kings' trust of the foreigners that eventually subjugated them for centuries.

The sparrows are very finicky and don't come too close. Their necks and eyes constantly rotate in every plane of motion. Their smartness shows up in their food hunting. The pigeons peck big crumbs into smaller ones, but never bite crumbs by holding in their beaks. They basically eat right where the food is found. Often, a tiny sparrow would fly into a bunch of pigeons, pounce upon a crumb right in front of them and fly away with it. After settling on a boundary wall, it enjoys eating it without any distraction.

The tiny ants are marvels of nature! Unless the food is dropped in their caravan path and not too far from their smell region, they do not run up to it. But the tiniest pieces of crumbs that are hardly visible to the naked eyes, they would carry them in their invisible mouths all the way into the crevices.

The caravan path of ants is never a straight line, but it is a smooth curve. The 90% of the ants suddenly stop and reverse their steps. It seems that only the adventurous amidst them go beyond a certain point to explore and scout information. It is really amusing to observe an ant and see how it 'greets' every ant that it encounters coming from the opposite direction. It is not slowed down, as humans would do. Actually, I know my childhood friend, Bal Krishan, who used to tag along with every friend to the consternation of his waiting parents.

Ants are incredible in relative strength. For instance, if human legs could move with the same frequency, as that of the ants, then humans will be running at supersonic speed of 800 mph. An ant can pull the weight 100 times of its weight! A big chunk of crumb that could not enter into the fissure they would first chisel it down. Each creature has a unique prowess that defines it. Any hierarchical classification of creatures is myopic. **Enlightenment comes in bits and pieces, and at times, when it is least expected.**

(June 25, 2006)

COMMENTS

1. Satish; I think this one was the best you have written yet. Very descriptive words, relatable story and excellent meaning. Thx. **Steve**

2. Dear brother, fine. I just enjoyed your reflection on pigeons, sparrows & ants. Anything in nature teaches us if we keep open our mind. Thank you for a fine reflection & information (speed of ant!!!).—**Soori**

3. This one was good Nana, and I liked the final line because it summed up the entire thing well. **Anjali**

4. You surely enjoy Life and Nature. **Subhash**

5. Thank you for the thought provoking piece. Very poetic, fine imageries . . . . yes, a person who has an eye to see can learn a lot from nature . . . . You deserve a lot of kudos. **Abraham**

TO BE OR NOT TO BE . . . .

Yesterday, two streams of thoughts converged. The number one was a young female calling the Radio Advice Host, Dr Laura Schlesinger (Noon-3 PM/ PST). Her question was: She was being pressured by her family to be 'given away' in marriage by her biological father—rather than the foster father, who had raised her since troubled teen years. She revealed that her biological father had sexually molested her two older sisters and her mother knew it. Yet, the sisters and mother wanted the biological father honored by not only inviting him at the wedding but also 'give her away'. Dr Laura is a principled moral person with an incredibly incisive mind and clarity for which I admire her. She blasted the family and admonished the caller for even thinking of it.

The second thing happened in the evening. My wife and her brother's family were gathering at my daughter's poolside for swimming and snacking. When asked about my joining it, my wife spoke up, "You know, he never goes for swimming!" This scenario is repeated every other week during summer. She knows that I am an avid swimmer in open oceans, large lakes, running brooks, ever since I learnt swimming in 1950, in the waters of Bathinda canal.

Where is the connection between the two scenarios? First, going back to Dr Laura's Show, it is to be understood that the callers are screened for various reasons. The questions of general/burning interest are mostly responded. Having seen, read and heard of growing cases of incestuous relations between natural fathers and daughters, real brothers and sisters in the US, I have tried to understand the dynamics of social life.

There is a thin veneer between such relationships, and once that is pierced, it is all over. In Urdu language, there is a word *HAYA* (means modesty+shame) for it. How can the ogling males turn around their carnal desires from fulsome women in string bikinis spread over lounge chairs or dipped in water to their sisters, daughters, granddaughters in the same pool area? Or conversely, can a male really look at all the women in the pool the way he looks at his sister, daughter and granddaughter? Incidentally, in the domain of public sensuality, Hinduism is miles away from other religions.

It is not a question of being hot blooded or not. In fact, this ultra exhibitionism of females has de-sexed the males and further feminized them. Men and women by their instincts are out there to score on each other. In an unguarded pool/beach environment, it takes one split moment to ignite the flame. No one party is to be totally blamed.

Understanding the power of sex, the Hindu scriptures are very clear about it. **They go to the extent of forbidding mother and son staying together in dark**—the most pious relation between two humans in every culture. The darkness is not of the absence of sun. It is the darkness that clouds the mind in sexual frenzy: senses are eclipsed, eyes don't see, ears don't hear and intellect cannot discriminate right from wrong. A beast inside is let loose to go on passionate rampage for a few minutes.

As I thoughtfully age, Shakespeare's famous line: **Nothing is good and nothing is bad, but thinking makes it so,** reveals new dimensions of human understanding. Twenty-five years ago, during a visit to India, while discussing bride burning over dowries, a Hindu MD remarked, "A permanent solution of this problem is to legitimize marriages between real brothers and sisters, Then the mother-in-law, also being mother, won't cause any dowry problems!" At that point, having lived in the US for only ten years, this remark shook my moral moorings. Seven years ago, at another meeting in India, when I asked him if he still remembered saying it—yes, he said!

In the present USA, the issues of same sex marriages and abortion (corollaries of growing sexual liberation) have vertically divided the nation. What was considered abominable or criminal is being eroded and relaxed. The American Library Association doesn't want to filter pornography on the library computers. The researchers in American Psychological Associations believe that pedophilia is not criminal. It is called the freedom of expression and strongly defended by the American Civil Liberty Union. In such an environment, a person of my values is viewed as an oddity, despite the massive data on traditional families breaking apart.

The change, flexibility and adaptability are all good buzzwords. We all change with time, sometimes quickly for convenience or with internal discipline. **But life is equally defined by its fixed points; the lofty ideals and uncompromising standards**. I have extensively traveled, read deeply and lived actively for more than six decades. My disinclination towards an extended pool/tub party is because I think it is a visual orgy.

It reminds me of my regular swimming in a pool (20'x40') on the top of a 14-storey apartment tower in Kuala Lumpur, Malaysia, in 1998. Soon after returning from work, I would fix a drink (gin and orange juice) and sip it while swimming alone in the pool under the open sky. Once in a while, two young women in the water would add sensuality to the pool. But once the number increased to 5-7, I would jump out and leave!

It is not a question of hormones raging out of control during teen years and becoming dormant during geriatric phase. The moral of the story of sage (Rishi) Vishwamitra/Bill Clinton is that a Maneka (mythological temptress/ Monica will eventually bring a man perched on high moral grounds to his/ her (?) knees. That is her **DHARAM** (basic nature) to live for and live by! In the movie, **Gandhi**, Gandhi cautions a female journalist," Don't try to seduce me."

What is my bottom line on 'bare' bottoms and bosoms in family pool parties? Life is separated from death and destruction by only one tenth of a second, when driving at 80—90 MPH and one tenth of a foot standing on the edge of a precipice. It is safer to drive on a racecourse at 120 MPH, do the sky diving, or bungee jumping. What a **Reflection** it has turned out to be!

(July 20, 2006)

COMMENTS

1. Laura a principled moral person! You must be kidding. Did you see her topless pictures and read about her relationship with married man. You think families did not break before the ACLU existed or feminism started? As about sex it is in head. Do you think incest does not occur in conservative countries like Saudi Arabia or India? I also puzzled by your attitude to sex. You glorify ogling nude women in Las Vegas and in this article you have turned 180 degree. **Rahul**

2. Satish, Excellent thoughts in this one. And you didn't even have to use Vegas "no ifs, ands, or butts" billboards or taxi signs.

In Christian scripture the 10 commands say "Don't commit adultery" and the Pharisees, the pious leaders of the Jews who thought they could do everything but have intercourse with women crowed about how well they followed the laws. Jesus came and told them, "You have heard don't commit adultery but I tell you, whoever even looks at a woman with lust in his heart has ALREADY committed adultery in his mind." There is a point where looking or accidental seeing turns into desiring, lingering and lusting. It is that point we must avoid but prevention like you describe. I would even go so far as to condemn sexual education and co-ed learning as being too far, but then again, I want to go back to arranged marriages too.

Thanks again for coming and sharing with our church, you gave our people wider looks into people and culture that many have yet to experience. They often forget that there are people who earnestly follow different paths than their own. You gave them a lot of food for thought and fodder for discussion. I was asked how I would answer your challenge that your "experience tells you" that you are correct and on the right path . . . here is my answer: I came out of a movie one time that was extremely well done, it was glorious in cinematography, the story captured you and pulled you in, my emotions came to the surface as I laughed and cried at various parts. Next to me was a middle-aged couple who discussed the movie as they walked in the warm night to their car. The movie had given them such comfort because it showed the afterlife and they had just lost their twenty-something child to an accident. They hugged each other thanking the creators of that movie for showing them the beauty of death and the afterlife. This movie was a wonderful experience for them, and it was a moving experience for me but it all was DEAD WRONG and even EVIL in its intent to deceive.

Satish, experience is the shakiest of pillars to build on. We used to turn in circles with our forehead pressed against a broom handle as a game. When you could do it no more you would try to walk normal. The experience was of the world spinning out of control and you could no longer stand much less walk straight. But it was all in your mind (or your inner ear actually) All of our senses can so easily be deceived by clever photos, videos, games, amusement rides and even writings that experience becomes poor substitute for truth.

St. Augustine has given me my creed for life which you will see on my website and in my writings. In Latin he stated: "Credo put intelligam" or in English "I believe, in order that I might understand" Belief MUST come before experience or you have no context to understand this crazy world. **Steve Wunderink**

3. *Yes, it is sometimes very difficult to draw a line of demarcation between morality and immorality. Probably it depends. What is moral is immoral for another. It also varies from place to place and culture to culture. In the Old Testament there is an instance of two daughters sleeping with their father for the purpose of procreation! Read "Song of Solomon" in the Bible. Some say it is very near to pornography . . . Perhaps Shakespeare is right. It is all in the mind. Hemingway also said" If you feel good after doing a thing, it is moral, if you don't feel good . . . it is immoral . . . Anyway, life is full of contradictions . . . and the mystery and enigma of life still perturbs me . . . Why all this "Tamasa"?! Keep writing.* Thanks . . . Thought provoking! **Abraham**

I wrote: Thanks! The paradox of living lies in chemical composition and that is **constantly changing** in a person. That is what defines his moods, gross actions and repentances etc. This is strictly at the individual level, in the confines of bedroom. As soon as an action touches the second person (that it must by its very nature), it becomes a belief, stand and action of two!

There is no common chemical composition of two except perhaps of math or rhetoric! Now you keep on adding one person at a time of different age and sex of a community and imagine/grapple the scenario. Any emotion or benchmark of moral or legality **changes** from one person to two persons, and many persons. This problem is so identical to Many Body Gravitational Problem in mathematical physics! This problem is well posed, but defies a solution.

Steve wrote: It is a paradox but it is also oxymoronic. There MUST by definition be something beyond us, us as individuals and us as society. There MUST be something beyond our nature, something UN-natural or something SUPER-natural. There MUST be because if what is in us is all there is we sink into a miry mess of mediocrity. An external source needs to define what is "good" or "right" or even "bad" or "wrong". We cannot define these ourselves because it would have no meaning to others it must be defined from the outside. Picture the World Cup where there are no external, arbitrary officials, head butts would lead to fists, fists to knives, knives to guns. Goals become whatever you would like to define them as. Winning and losing would have no meaning, the "game' itself would have no meaning and be reduced to a miry mediocrity of men in small shorts.

Mathematics, yes! A perfect example of laws and rules outside the individual but math, while it can impact the quality and quantity of life, can never answer the truly important questions of life. "As iron sharpens Iron . . . " **Steve**

TWO SLICES OF ONE LIFE

The fundamental emotional states of life begin and end at the same level of consciousness. Strangely enough, they converge at the extreme ends of a **linear** life span. Some also describe it as **cyclic**. The enigma is that in between the two states, the life pulsates with zillions of varied experiences.

The other day, we were watching a family video of a dance and music function during a typical Indian wedding. Indian wedding atmosphere is very informal for everyone to have fun and laughter. There was an eruption of applause when the 90-year old matriarch, sitting amongst her entourage of progeny, kicked into the festive mood. She can barely walk. All she did was to gracefully stand up, slowly turned her hands above the head into a dance movement and smiled. Everyone clapped and profusely greeted her.

The very next day, at another family gathering, our 13-month grandson Anex (Taj) was playing with me—more appropriately, I was roughing him up. After a few minutes, I stood him up on the wooden floor. Well, he turned a small angle and took 4-5 steps for the first time! Perhaps, surprised by his new achievement, he quickly slumped down in his comfort zone. By then, everyone had noticed him—cheered and hugged him.

The connection between the two is obvious. At the initial end of life, the first step is a big moment for the memory books. The 'last' step is big too at the terminal end. The coordination of muscles and sensory controls that gradually appear in the beginning stages of life, begin to disappear gradually at the terminal end of life. It is a stark reality and common fate of mankind. With exercise, diet and fitness routines one may delay physical dependency, or shorten it a bit, but can never eliminate it! The last geriatric year or two are as solid in dependency as the first two years of infancy.

Four years ago, an assisted living complex opened half a mile from our home. Its sidewalk sign welcomes visitors for the tours of the facility. I see it every time I walk or drive by it. But I tell myself that it has nothing to do with me! My curiosity being constant about places, people and ideas, last week, I asked myself, "Are you scared to visit it?" When the answered came out a no, I turned around and went inside.

I got a cordial welcome. The residents are between 60-90 years in age. Most of them have lost part of their memory; because of particular diseases, strokes or accidents. The senior institutions are integral to the US life styles, as are its educational institutions—like Harvard and Stanford. Loneliness is a part of life, as infants in childcare centers, or as fossilized seniors in assisted living. With the fast pace of life and couples working, there is no family time and space for the infants, or elderlies, who don't want to lose their prized 'privacy'! Human life has evolved, mutated and survived. **Continuing to have fun and not taking oneself too seriously is a gateway to its peaceful passage**.

(Aug 16, 2006)

COMMENTS

1. Bravo! So well said. Reminded me of Shakespeare's seven stages of man. Here are the last 2 lines from that poem:
   Is second childishness and mere oblivion,
   Sans teeth, sans eyes, sans taste, sans everything.
   Regards, **Rahul**

2. Dr. Bhatnagar: I read every posting and particularly from you that embodies an in-depth wisdom and linked to our legendary culture. Your current theme reminds me of our "Mahavarata" mythology that has depicted the human life as a cycle that begins with our birth and end in old age that have a lot of similarity but metabolically different—the first one is more anabolic and the last one is more catabolic. However, I enjoyed the deep underlying philosophy in **"TWO SLICES OF ONE LIFE." Gouranga Saha**

3. I liked the juxtaposition of the child and the 90-year-old matriarch. The "cheer" of the old is a rare phenomenon nowadays. I daily observe the old women who are our neighbour, neglected by her husband and son, living all alone. One can read the story of agony on her wrinkled face. Back in our country also, things are no better. Dementia is a common disease nowadays. Old age homes are coming up all over. Children are in USA or other gulf countries. Once in a while they visit their old parents who are taken care of by strangers. Lifestyle has changed entirely. The beauty of joint family system in our country is mostly out of date. I often wonder about the futility of all these. Are God's ways so mysterious! Keep writing. My grandson (6 months) is sitting on my lap while I scribble these lines, and he is restless. So let me stop. Thanks. **Abraham**

LIFE MOVES ON WITH CHANGES

At times, the ability and desire to change habits and life styles are incredible in human beings. Sixteen years ago, during a routine check up, I was advised to be on blood pressure (BP) pills for the rest of my life. It shocked me, as I thought myself reasonably healthy. Immediately, on the advice of a physician friend, I threw away the saltshaker from the dining table. Also, taking raw garlic a few times a week helped in bringing the BP down. Likewise, when people are stunned to discover after a blood profile about the onset of diabetes, they cut down on sweets, and switch to 'boring' foods that they had despised before. The drastic changes in daily routines are particularly brought around after heart attacks and surgeries.

By extending the definition of relationships to objects, places and ideas, such instances are turning points in life. However, people are unwilling to accept when conflicts occur between individuals. On looking back at my span of six decades, some relationships have turned upside down. The bitterness continues to simmer under the skin. It is unhealthy.

Last week, during such a scenario, it flashed me that why individuals don't admit temper blowouts, as time to change behaviors. No one wants to go back to the habits that caused high BP, diabetes, or plaque in the arteries. The reason is simple: we all want to live longer. There is a new beginning after a health setback. I know a close friend who suffered heart attack at the age of 30. Immediately, he quit heavy smoking and late night heavy meals. He switched to bland diet and started an exercise regimen—including long hikes that he used to ridicule. He lived for 34 more years. Had he continued his old ways, he would have checked out before 40, perhaps, from a massive heart attack.

In human confrontation, life is not immediately at stake. But it should be considered as the beginning of a new phase. Harping on 'good-old-times' is fruitless. Perhaps, they were not that good. Otherwise, the seismic cracks would not have come around. Reconciliation is good, but it can never and should not bring back the 'good old' spirit.

Memory plays a tremendous role in relationships. During teen years, we all fight and mend with friends. The future was vastly open and exciting that bickering in a short past was quickly forgotten. It changes, as families come into the picture and professional ambitions become paramount. Once you turn 60, the time zones are reversed; future appears shorter and worrisome, but past comforting!

The desire for getting back to 'good-old-days' is indeed, a cause of new unhappiness. The analysis of happiness is marvelous. We think that one's happiness lies in the pocket of the other person, or even in a place or thing. It may be true to a little extent, but untrue at large. Its proof lies in the collective experience of mankind. Life is a long string of shiny pearls identified with moments of joy and sorrow. **A common paradox of human life is when memories of a tragedy turn into a blessing after some time, and conversely!**

(Oct 11, 2006)

COMMENTS

1. Dear Satish: I enjoyed your this write-up immensely. What a good stream of reflections! Regards, **Bhu Dev Sharma**

2. The essential needs of humans seem to be often ignored these days in place of artificial and concocted desires. What about the most important needs of: 1. respect for feelings 2. appreciation 3. admiration 4. Affection 5. consideration 6. courtesy 7. kindness 8. Generosity. Oh, if only people would realize that all people need the above. These are the building bricks of a human personality and would bring peace and contentment to our lives. I'm a voice in the wilderness . . . . but the most important is respect for feelings. We all have feelings, from little tiny babies to old, decrepit 100-year-old men and women. Feelings, feelings, feelings get hurt so needlessly these days. It makes me sad to see feelings hurt. Love, **Dutchie**

LIVING IS AN ART

Beauty of life shines out in its paradoxes too. This is triggered by a key write-up in the current issue (12/06) of the *AARP Bulletin* (American Association of Retired Persons). It is about a 68-year old clay potter, who survived a killer cancer detected when he was 57. For thirty years prior, he owned a law firm and rolled in wealth. During hospitalization and rehab, he discovered new directions, and thanked cancer for it! He quit law forever.

My thoughts ricocheted in various directions. One was while growing up in Bathinda, my hometown in India, I saw potters shaping all kinds of earthenwares. In the biggest house in the neighborhood lived an illiterate, dark, and burly *kumhar* (potter) named, Mangal. In India, the profession of potting still belongs to the 'backward' classes! Mangal was a millionaire of his time and his young and fair wife was always covered with gold. Still, they were not socially acceptable. Even today, in big cities of India, one finds entire families living on roadsides in thatched huts and engaged in making and painting varied ceramic toys and idols. Their living condition is a picture of misery and unhappiness.

Happiness (?) or satisfaction (?) in life does not reside **forever** in potting clay or practicing law, if all creative energies are directed through one outlet only. It is true in any intense and passionate relationship—whether with a person, place, or thing. Blocking out the rest of the world creates a vacuum that eventually collapses under external forces. **This is a heavy price that great creative minds have paid in every age and society**. Man, naturally born with many talents, cannot be reduced to one dimension for too long.

Yesterday, I got an e-mail about a popular book, *The Monk Who sold his Ferrari*. It is on the same theme of a profiled New York attorney, who quits it all after a massive heart attack. Soon after, he roams India and discovers 'happiness'. At the same time we know hoards of Indian monks visiting the US and seeking financial support for their projects. I enjoy paradoxes in life, as they also provide material for my Honors Seminar, *Paradoxes in Arts, Science and Mathematics!*

Six years ago, I attended a course on artificial intelligence (AI) taught by a philosophy professor. I was curious, as AI mainly belongs to computer science and neuroscience. In that class, Joe Marino remains unforgettable.

He is one the top heart surgeons in Las Vegas. He came from Italy in 1968. He confided how he was burnt out—a syndrome of modern professionalism. He found 'satisfaction' in studying philosophy! Again, how many read philosophy for it? My wife did MA in philosophy from Punjabi University, Patiala at the persuasion of a philosophy professor, who was a neighbor and landlady too!

Tragedies are to be understood as the turning points of life. Life is like a water stream that changes its course when hit by boulders, falls and canyon walls. Of course, on a geologic scale, a stream also changes the entire landscape, as it meanders its way out!

(Dec 06, 2006)

COMMENTS

1. Yes, life is full of paradoxes. Very few turn the crisis into an opportunity. Others plunge into the labyrinth of despair and for them, "Life is a tale told by an idiot full of sound and fury signifying nothing" I often wonder what this is "tamasha" called life! Yet I enjoy the enigma, perhaps it is the enigma of life that gives beauty to it. **Abraham**

2. How true. Thanks for the moment. Whatever you are doing, seeing, hearing, touching, smelling, eating, or saying, realize your essential nature as pure Consciousness. This is the way to liberation, aka happiness. Possession of a Ferrari or getting rid of it by itself does not lead to happiness. **Ved P. Sharma**

3. Dear Tauji, I enjoyed your prose and believe in your philosophy. Please add my email in your mailing list. My chachaji always used to tell me about your intellect and your pure thoughts. With regards, **Ashish Saxena**

TO BE, OR NOT TO BE

How brittle your personality is—defines your old age. The lonesome urbanites are very brittle—physically, socially, and emotionally. In the present US, people don't like to be called old even when the age touches a number. A popular cliché is that one is as old as one 'feels', as if all the 'feeling' thermostats are fully operational. Old age is simply the last phase of 10-15 years of one's life span, which one does not know.

In old age, the bones break down during ordinary physical activities and impact. It is now explained as a medical problem, osteoporoses. My 42-year old sedentary daughter has broken the same ankle twice in one year! She did not hit any object, stumble, or twist. The inconvenience of three weeks at home, work, and doctor visits have become integral part of a fast life style. It is happening in countries like India. I have never seen bigger crowds in waiting rooms of any physicians in the US, as that of orthopedic surgeons. Patients are seen sitting outside the waiting rooms, and not complaining about it.

The broken bones are re-fixed after a few weeks, but more fragile are the social relations. Listening to the talk radios, reading newspaper columns, and personally witnessing relationships in our large circle of friends and relatives, they make me wonder at the lower thresholds of differences. The irony of social snap-down is that it is irreversible amongst the oldies! A few days ago, at a social, two ladies wondered at the other two, who were amicably talking with each other—despite their fighting a couple of years ago! A reconciliation, 'making it up', or 'cleaning the air', is not in the air any more.

Benjamin Franklin (1706-90), in his Autobiography that I just finished, writes of his several associations started as adult, but lasting for life. **That is the only sentence he has repeated in several places**! However, he did avoid one person who was vexation to his spirit of entrepreneurship. Death is nothing but snapping of all the ties one by one.

Being brittle is tragic at the emotional level. During old age, in the US, when the children are long gone and have their own children, the two lives are back to Square One. They are left to feel 'emotional' about each other till one is Gone. The frailty and fragility of spousal tie also peaks at this stage. During the passionate years of youth even a big outburst was cooled off in the bed. With inflated egos in old age, an emotional crack comes quicker and lasts longer. Moreover, physical cuts and bruises stop healing up fast.

Last week, a defamatory e-mail from an outcaste angered us; though it came in a pattern of behavior. I kept quiet, but my wife reacted over it. Eventually, it engulfed us in flair-up of our tempers. The invisible emotional scars are more permanent than any scars of broken bones or bonds. At least, one spouse must keep quiet for sanity to swing back. According to ancient Hindu wisdom, the men are supposed to 'leave' homes and engage in greater causes of life. Now I understand why the couples in the US divorce in old ages. With all buffers gone, thresholds lowered, life in old age is like rowing without oars.

(Jan 26, 2007)

RIVER OF LIFE

"Was he the only son?", inquired my sister, when I told her about the tragic death of our cousin's 24-year old son, in India. It was caused by electrocution from a pedestal fan right in his home. She added that in a modern trend of having nuclear families, the parents must be prepared that their only child may be prematurely taken away by a random accident, act of violence, or disease. A memorial ceremony is set for tomorrow.

After the conversation, I walked up to a mortuary—near home. While strolling along the aisles of the burials and reading inscriptions on the headstones, it flashed that because of a Meta 'sequential' nature of human existence, **every life touches some lives, but no life touches every life tangibly.** At one end of a burial site was the grave of a 3-day old infant. One wonders how such a small life could leave any mark—is a perfect example. **"The angels in the heaven were so lonely that they called him back,"** was engraved on its granite stone. For a moment, my thoughts were frozen in a track. All visions and talks about legacy seemed egoistic and amount to naught in a long haul.

My brooding continued. **Does a life really touch other lives all the time?** With withering nature of memory, I don't think there is a life that does it for 24/7. Deeper an interactive experience, the shorter may be the duration of its action on the mind. One can only say that overall, a particular life touched a few lives in a positive manner. On the other hand, if the impact is overall negative, then it is publicly over.

As I contemplatively glanced over the gravestones around me, I asked myself: would I like to be 'visited' like this? The question of the disposal of the 'dead' body has come up a few times. Certainly, whatever my body parts are of any medical use would be taken out, as I have signed up for organ donation. My wish is that the 'remains' be cremated as soon as possible. If anyone did not see me when recently alive, or have not known me through my *Reflections*, then I don't want to be 'viewed' after it is all over with the body.

With all considerations, the best disposition of the dead body is through high-tech electric cremation. It can heat up to 7000 degree F that the body literally evaporates leaving minimum ashes; no sentimentalism with the ashes. Let the ashes be spread right away in a nearby desert area or a wash, but no holding of it in an urn. People's visits to the graves last only for a few years. Once the wave of the knowers has passed, the number trickles down to zero. With cremation of the body, any kind of physical controversy is gone too. I want people to go back to their normal lives as soon as possible.

Recently, my students and I estimated that at least 100 billion people have lived on Planet Earth during the last 1000 years alone. The number, 100,000,000,000 still may not convey its magnitude. But come to think, that the present population of the world is over 5 billion. Taking into consideration of billion-year age of Planet Earth, gazillions of human beings have come and gone 'leaving' no trace or record behind!

(Mar 17, 2007/Mar, 2012)

COMMENTS

1. I agree with your last will and testament and I am of the exact same view. I am quoting some translated verses from Bachchan's (my other favorite poet) famous Madhushala:

"Yama will come as the wine-maiden and bring his black wine,
Drink, and know no more consciousness, O carefree one.
This is the ultimate trance, the ultimate wine-maiden and the ultimate goblet.
O traveler, drink judiciously, for you will never find the tavern again.
Touch not my lips with Tulsi, but with the goblet, when I die.
Touch not my tongue with the Ganga waters, but with wine, when I die.
When you bear my corpse, pallbearers, remember this!
Call not the name of God, but call to the truth that is the tavern.
Weep over my corpse, if you can weep tears of wine.
Sigh dejectedly for me, if you are intoxicated and carefree.
Bear me on your shoulders, if you stumble drunkenly along.
Cremate me on that land, where there once was a tavern.
Pour on my ashes, not ghee, but wine.
Tie to a vine of grapes, not a water pot, but a wine-goblet.
And when, my darling, you must call guests for the ritual feast,
Do this—call those who will drink and have the tavern opened for them.
If anyone asks my name, say it was, "The Drunkard".
My work? I drank and passed the goblet to everyone.
O Beloved, if they ask my caste, say only that I was mad.
Say my religion worshipped goblets and then chant with your rosary,
    "The tavern, the tavern!"
O son, raise not water at my final rites, but wine in your palms.
And sit somewhere, having filled the Ganga with wine.
If you can wet the earth somewhere, my soul will be satisfied.
Offer your libations to your ancestral spirits by reading repeatedly,
    "The tavern, the tavern." **Rahul**

2. Dear Satish, Yes, I don't think of Mr. Norman Slater 24/7. He was a deep and profound influence on my life, my thinking and my personality. He's been dead for almost 15 years and I miss him, his thoughts, his kindness, his wisdom, his honesty, his peculiarities, his visions and his respect, appreciation, affection, courtesy, consideration, his wonderful treatment of me for me. He wanted to be buried and I did bury him. Did I visit the grave? Well, while attending the funeral for a cousin I did and when I took a friend to visit her son and husband's grave I did. The visit to Norman's

grave did nothing for me. It was just a piece of ground with his name on a flat plate. Too bad for me. Love, **Dutchie**

3. This write up was indeed thought provoking, though it gave an eerie sensation within me. Yes, life is so evanescent and yet man thinks that he is going to be here for eternal . . . and that he is the Lord of the Universe! An awareness of death is a very healthy attitude, I often think . . . Perhaps it makes you a humble and nice human being . . .

Back in Kerala, I remember as a young boy, I used to watch funeral processions with great curiosity. Even now, I vividly remember the words written on the black coffin in big Malayalam letters . . . the translation . . . "Today I am leaving, tomorrow you are following me"!

It is really a great gesture and humanitarian act to donate one's organs for medical research or if they are of any use to any one . . . after all once the life/soul is out of the body . . . cremation/funeral/memorial services all those stuff are just formalities . . . and who cares! . . . Within no time one is out of mind . . . "Out of sight, out of mind" . . . Yes, it should be like that . . . and Life should go one in spite of you . . . and that I think is the beauty of Life! May you live long and keep writing "Reflections". Good luck. **Abraham**

4. I thought I better let you know what I have thought of often, that how much I appreciate your phone calls and these reflections. It is strange though that all the years that I was married to your friend, we never talked to each other. Thank you so much for your concern. I do believe that people come in one's life for a reason. We may not know the reason right away, though. My illness has brought several people in my life, they have become a source of comfort and support. I feel so blessed in my life. Thank you. **Dinesh**

PERSONAL COMMENTS

SLICING AWAY REINCARNATION

In general, we think age wise i.e. our thoughts are functions of age. It is like people—living in a neighborhood, have comparable income. Another scenario: people, writing children's books or directing children movies, understand kids. Furthermore, we do not think too far from what we have already experienced. Quantum leaps in one's thoughts look exceptions only to the others.

Certainly, I could not imagine the states of mind of a 67-year-old person, when I was 17. In fact, I never even had it as mental exercise 50 years ago. What will be my thoughts when I grow to be 67 old? Now that I am 67, and I 'know' how I was once one year old—66 years ago. An elementary exercise is to recall the ideas of each year. Based upon it, can I write a *Reflection* for my 15-year old grandson? This question is really pertinent in the context of reincarnation. How would I remember my memories of my 'previous' birth, if I cannot remember what happened a few years ago?

This is an interesting mental game to play. Communication experts tell that after listening, one cannot reproduce the text after an hour! Once I tried to write down what had gone into my mind 24 hours earlier. I could hardly fill three pages. Human memory is selective. Also, it constantly erases bits of unused information. Special events—like tragedies, disappointments, betrayals, and acts of ungratefulness, cut deep grooves in the mental drive that they last longer.

Of course, human memory drive can crash too, and lose all the data. Psychiatrists can help in the recovery process, as some IT experts are thriving in the business of retrieving data from the CD crashes. They charge a couple thousand dollars, as their clients are mostly company CEOs!

My ability of recall is really incredible. At this age, it seems to function at two extremes. I can't outrightly tell what shirt I was wearing yesterday, though I am not a sloppy dresser—relatively speaking. I don't pickup my clothes thoughtlessly. Another common scenario is that I go to a room to pick up an item, but do something else. It is only in the second visit that I complete the task. However, I can survey a part of world history with reasonable accuracy.

I won't know of my 'reincarnated' life, as I won't remember a thing. This is also based on an assumption that human beings are reincarnated into human beings. Given a conscious choice (by whom??), I would love to reincarnate into a lion, an eagle, or a shark. The underlying unity of all entities implies that one life ought to be transferable into the other. If it is like an Axiom of Choice in mathematics, then I would like to reincarnate as a rock or tree, as narrated to in the Hindu epic, **Ramayana**.

The concept of reincarnation is like that of mermaids—coming out of man's fancy imagination since time immemorial. A lesson of history is that a person has never taken a birth in same physical identity. However, the records, of previous birth memories of rare people, from every land on earth, continue to baffle the public. The rest are only statistical conclusions.

(June 07, 2007)

THE NEW AGE YOGIS

The modern communication technologies have transformed people into yogis of a kind. The scientists and inventors are linear yogis anyway. Yogi is supposedly a person, outwardly unaware of immediate surroundings, yet sensitive to the **Butterfly Effects** in the universe. While growing up in Bathinda (BTI), we often teased kids who lived in their own worlds. In the advertisements of mind related health products, the yogis, sitting in lotus postures with eyes closed, are iconic images in the world around.

Since **9/11 Attack on America**, one spends more time in the gate lounges of the airlines than in the flights. First, you arrive at least an hour before flight and then add an hour in 50% of the cases, when the flight is delayed. The travelers are essentially captives for hours. Well, that is what recently happened to me for one-hour flight from Las Vegas to San Jose, but I ended up spending two hours in waiting. It does not bother me anymore, as I carry stuff for reading, writing and munching pleasures. However, no less, I enjoy observing a variety of people seen only at the airports. It is a wondrous spectacle! The human eyes cannot distinguish individual cows, ants and birds in their, herds, colonies and flocks. May be, for these creatures we, all human beings, look alike too!

Confined for an hour, Americans mind with their own business. Before the laptop age, travelers in the trains, buses, and planes were seen reading books, magazines and newspapers. It is a US cultural trait—not witnessed during India travels. Now most men, women too, are seen hooked up with their laptops, i-pods, i-phones and other electronic gadgetries. Most US public places provide internet hook-ups or wireless zones.

When a person, a seat away, suddenly spoke up, I thought he was addressing me. I turned towards him, but he continued to speak straight. For a moment, it appeared spooky, but soon I realized that he had a phone system that freed his hands with a microphone plug inserted into the ear away from me. Like a yogi, he can talk with anyone on the planet!

A person in a high tech age, wants to remain independent from his immediate neighbors, but at the same time, wants the entire world on the palm of his hands. It reminded me of a *'sadh'* (half yogi!) in BTI. His abode was on the outskirts of the town. The rumors of an underground chamber of his dwelling added a layer of mystique to his persona. Once a month or two, he used to walk into the town wearing a long ochre kurta with a short underneath. The years of walking over long distances had curved his legs like bows! I never saw him speaking with anyone. It is the same for the modern high-tech yogis. Their backs and shoulders are stooped down after years of bending over tiny screens and keys!

The holy places of the Hindus in India are known for ascetics of various orders, outfits, garbs, facial make-ups, names and fames. No two yogis are seen talking with each other, though they claim to be connected with the worlds above and below. What a confluence of technologies of mind and matter. Setting up a bridge between the two is a goal of my life!

(Aug 03, 2007)

COMMENTS

1. Thank you for this reflection; I really enjoyed it. Sincerely, **Renato**

2. Have heard jokes about Zen Buddhists, who seem to be similarly meditative. Here's one: The ZB tells the Hot Dog Vendor, "Make me one with everything." Impressed, the HDV says, "That will be two and a half dollars." The ZB pays with a twenty, and waits. Eventually, he asks for his change. HDV: "Change comes only from within," **Looy**

3. Dear Satish, A keen observer, you. Love this one too. Images pop up in my mind as I was reading it. Thank you very much. Love, **Dutchie**

4. Good one, Satish Jee! Technologies of mind Technologies of matter — a bridge between them? What a thought provoking idea!!!!!! Always, **Manmohan**

5. *Hum wahan hai jahan se humko bhi*
   Kuch hamari khabar nahin aati (Ghalib) **Rahul**

6. I have highlighted one of your observations that has always continued to amaze me . . . . no two humans look exactly the same. **RAJA**

7. Hi Satish: Now that I have read your 'reflection' on contemporary technology-oriented yogi, I feel I am behind times. An interesting piece it is. **Moorty**

8. While reading the write up, I felt myself as a 'new age yogi" . . . of course in a very "humble way . . . one day the computer didn't work . . . felt really unrest. as though I was in a loss.! I liked the expression "butterfly effect" and the "technologies of mind and matter" **Abraham**

9. Right on, or should I say spot one, Satish! Another alienating factor in the US is that people commute to work, solo, cooled by air conditioning and listening to the radio. They have no way to interact with other people even if they wanted to. **Dave Emerson**

10. Dear Satish, Your article of the new age yogis is a perfect observation of our society. In the modern age we have lost emotion & love. We are always calculated of profit & loss and always cautious of the job in hand and perpetual cautious us. Even on bed with the wife he has to take aid of

liquors and then sleep. He has even forgotten how to enjoy the delicacies of the food, because he is more cautious of the blood pressure and the diabetes tendency. In fact he is not a man but a machine without love & affection. Your Sincerely, **VED BHUSHAN**

PERSONAL REMARKS

A TRIANGLE OF SAVINGS, COMFORT AND SPENDING

Yesterday, my friend of 50+ years called me from India. Yes, we have kept a regular communication for all these years. For the last one year, he has been disgusted with his living environment. His diabetic problems seem now out of the charts, wife suffered a stroke last year and just broke her shoulder in a fall due to paralytic effects of the stroke.

Both of them lived happily in a small town Nahan till wife's medical treatment forced them to move to Ludhiana (LDH), where their son runs a good business. The son is divorced, but has the custody of two pre-teen kids. Since the son has a typical 9-9 day routine, the responsibilities of taking care of the kids and household have fallen on grandparents' ageing shoulders. Both loved walking, but are now handicapped. The air and noise pollution of industrialized LDH is making them miserable no less.

Life, towards the end of journey, takes strange turns and twists. My friend had retired in financial comfort. With right investments, he multiplied his fortune. I told him, "At the present state of health, you have no more than of five years to live. With a cash of Rs. 30 lakhs (3 million.) in a bank, and no debts, it is time to spend some savings on comforts. Hire a nurse and housemaid to take the burden off your shoulders. Move into a better housing development."

Another friend, in Ambala, literally lived for years on piles of squalor with his octogenarian mother in a dilapidated mansion. He declined to sell 1/5th of his plot for Rs 1 crore (10 m.)! Mother died 3 years ago, and he Followed her last year. He was a 'non-practicing' MD intellectual of a kind. It also reminds me of my father who owned a house and a big plot. During the last 2 years of his life, he struggled to balance his meager pension with household expenses. He did not sell a portion of a plot to alleviate the hardships during his last days.

There is an emotional attachment with whatever one accumulates in lifetime. I saw a 70-year old professor in India, who had piles of daily newspapers with red under linings. They are saved for future referencing! Besides fire hazard, they are worthless even for the junk buyers. Some people who grow out of poverty and struggle to make a decent life, it is natural to be attached to the hard-earned savings. Nevertheless, saving is for the rainy days and spending it during retirement for buying wellness and comforts serve its sole purpose. Overtly, at the same time, spending is perceived as dwindling of the funds. This is an eternal triangle of growing old!

The last couple of years of declining life are very complex, no matter how well one has maintained one's health and finances. Good management does not eliminate these problems, it only postpones them. On the other side, what is the point of leaving inheritance for the kids who are reasonably well off and provided with good opportunities to succeed. It piques me to hear or read a line from the present generation that 'the parents are wasting our inheritance'. I admire Americans, living their 70s and 80s, who splurge in wild pursuits to stretch their geriatric limits. There is nothing to lose or prove anymore! In this context, I loved a line in the movie, *Rambo*, watched last night; **Live for nothing, but die for something**!

(Feb 02, 2008)

COMMENTS

1. The more I muse through your reflections, the more I realize the importance of the way of life, thinking and living as detailed in the Bhagwad Geeta, Upanishad and Vedas, and made applicable to day to day life by Late Shri Pandurang Shastri Athavale (Dadaji). We feel very fortunate to be part of it. It takes a lot of wisdom, confidence in self and trust in God to realize that wealth is a means and not an end. A *Subahsheet* in *Sanskrit* comes to mind that says accumulated wealth has three ends *Bhog* (spent on self), Raja (taxes) *Stena (Chor*—Swindlers). The fourth option is to spend in on activities that foster gratefulness, selfless and intellectual love for God (*Dharma*). Keep them coming. **Hasmukh**

2. Bhatnagar Sahib: I find this reflection one of the most perceptive and insightful reflections. This couple came back from a European vacation. Friends asked where they had gone. We had gone to 'ski' was the response. "We did not know you ever skied." No. ski means Spend Kids' Inheritance. **Ved Sharma**

3. It only goes to show "do you want to live rich or die rich" **Pramod (Dr)**

4. My dear Bhatnagar Sahib; Namaste I just read all of these *Reflections* the other day. They transport me to another world (I may sound repetitive) and enjoyed every bit of them I never knew you had other (prosperous) friends in Ludhiana. I am living diametrically opposite life, one I do not have no savings and two whatever I earn I spend (often to the last penny, that is why you don't find pennies lying around in India) to make life more comfortable. I have been fortunate a friend cum student gave me a car and offered to maintain it as long as he can afford it and he often pays for the gas I need. Another student cum friend has given me a brand new house to live all built and painted (though small). He wanted to liberate me from paying a hefty (by my standards) rent every month. However I look forward to the time when you will publish your reflections. **Jagjeet**

5. Hope you are practicing this, Satish! **Hortense**

6. This one is really good. **Aniruddha**

ONE MORE DOWN!

All desires are never fulfilled. This common cliché has third grade math behind it. Simply compute the number of hours in life. Simply put, the number of desires can never exceed the number of hours. However, there is a philosophical touch to this paradigm. By reducing the number of desires to zero, the average time goes to infinity in a limit! Aside this paradoxical flash, there is an opposite scenario, when a cherished desire takes an unexplainable long time before it is realized. Only the beauty and diversity of life, and not-so-strong desire for it may explain it.

Yesterday, for the first time, I completed a scenic 15-mile loop in the Red Rock Canyon in cool desert air. Five years ago, a friend and I had quit after doing 2/3 of it. This time, we were a party of five between the ages of 50-75. Only 2-3 right persons are needed for its planning. Thirty-four years ago, when we moved to Las Vegas, a check mark was placed on it. The desire would flare up during drives and short hikes with out-of-town guests. This national park, only 25 miles away from home, like a girl next-door in youthful days, always teased me. A mountain range of the red face of this horseshoe park, extending on the west side of Las Vegas Valley, is visible from anywhere.

How come it took me so many years? On such a long hike at varying altitude of 3700' to 4700', one must never go alone, no matter how young and fit you are. This is a cardinal principle of 'professional' hikers. Though I love to walk my neighborhood streets and parks every day, wilderness hiking is a different ball game.

Most Indian wives in my generation are not into hikes. My wife hates even outdoor walking. On the flip side, it may be a recipe for a long married life! In Las Vegas, we have a large circle of close relatives and friends. Amongst Indians, weekend parties are the most popular social outlets. You can have 10 families over dinner on a short notice, but not a single person for any outdoor activity. Mindsets do not switch their polarities.

The pace of my hiking or walking does not distract me from reflecting. Yes, I had brief exchanges with others. Our rest stops were spaced every two hours. Quinine tonic water helped in avoiding leg cramps that generally start shooting after 5-6 hours. Three fruits, three candy bars and a small sandwich kept my metabolic furnace in good shape.

The only visible fatigue signs were the bright red soles of my feet when I took off thick hiking socks. I should have raised my legs during the breaks. Also, there were two big blisters on the balls right next to the big toes. This morning, I took my wife's insulin syringe and extracted all the fluids. Had I done it yesterday, the skin would not have extended. But the soles feel fine. Before going to bed, I had two Advils so that the unusual stretching of muscles does not prolong. Certainly, the memories of the loop will stretch out. During the hike, I called my son in California for planning the celebrations of his forthcoming 40th birth anniversary with a jog on this loop. Viva, Las Vegas!

(Apr 04, 2008)

COMMENTS

1. Dear Satish, This is one of your very best. It is vivid, heartfelt and full of sage ideas and opinions. Thanks, pal. Hugs, **Dutchie**

2. thanks for the "loopy Reflection" . . . it could be part of your autobiography when u plan to write one. **Abraham**

TO LIE, OR NOT TO LIE

'AENT BHALAA, SO BHALAA' is a common Hindi maxim in India. It has an exact analog in English; **'All's well, if ends well.'** That tells the universality of some human experiences in daily lives. I have believed in it, and felt comforted many a times during 'youthful' years. However, it has started losing its shine with time. With age, everyone becomes cynical to some extent. It happens when the outcomes of repeat experiences are naturally re-cycled in life. At times, blessed are those who have shorter memories!

It all started, when I sent my passport along with **seven** required documents for Bolivian Tourist Visa. The package was FedExed on Friday, May 16 with return postage paid. However, the passport with visa arrived only yesterday afternoon—Wednesday, May 28—after 12 days! On the 19th, before leaving Las Vegas on 22nd, I called the Los Angeles (LA) Consulate about not getting the visa. Their website claims, that within 24 hours, the tourist visas are processed, if documents are right and FedExed.

During May 19-28, I made several calls to the Consulate. There was always a different story, though the person was the same. I am sure of his identity from the voice. Yesterday morning, I had to 'risk' the visa by raising my voice against this inordinate delay and contradictions, and insisted upon speaking with the Consulate. Enough is enough!

In India, there is a saying that to cover one lie, ten lies are invented. The morale is to tell the truth in the first place. The most striking feature about the American way of life is the nth degree of truthfulness in public dealings. Customer Service is an American business invention, now getting popular worldwide. At any US public counter, one gets factual information. If it is not 100%, then he/she would simply say it coldly—I don't know. In countries—like India, a person, having only 10 % of facts, won't hesitate in claiming to know it all! In fact, he/she may be trying to be overly helpful. Culture plays a role too.

According to the FedEx tracking number, my package was delivered at the Consulate on Tuesday, 20th, not on Monday. It is weird, as the ordinary mail would reach LA in four days from LV. There is an added mystery to their operation. The Consulate did not use my return Fed Ex tracking number!

Consequently, the PC never showed any online activity on the return package while repeatedly being told, that it has been sent out.

Finally, it was my yelling that broke up one-half of the mystery, when the Consulate gave a tracking number that was different from mine. According to its log, the passport was picked up on Friday evening of May 23. It was in Memphis for a day, and the long weekend caused further delay. Instead of delivering it on Tuesday, it was done on Wednesday. The Consulate not telling truthfully, about the dispatch date, is Bolivian. What did they do about my prepaid number? Rather than opening a new can of inquiries, I would take respite from it—all is well, if it ends well.

(May 29, 2008)

ART AND LIFE OF DEAD TREES

"High altitude pine trees are beautiful when they are alive; they are beautiful when they are dying; they are beautiful when they are dead!" Thus, I was talking with myself while leisurely hiking in a national forest area, known as Mt Charleston, 35 miles away from Las Vegas. The pine trees, growing between 8000'-10,000', are irresistible to the senses. There was hardly any other noticeable flora. It must be due to the survival of the fittest. At high altitude, the harsh climate of severe snow and howling winds brings toughness in people, plants, and creatures. Lives are bound to be shortened. Men may escape the rigors of weather with climatic controls.

Today, we, a party of four, started the hike from 7700'. Soon we were paced apart. Being not a morning person, I quickly get out of breath, but watch about not losing it. My steps get shorter, as the climb gets steeper or rougher. There is a ***Hiking Paradox***. No matter how steep a climb is, one should never completely come to a stand still in order for the lungs to 'open up'. While catching on my breath, I still can enjoy the nature around me. The binoculars are my companions too. The distant mountain sides, rock formations, layered cracks, and caves, all come to life through binoculars! I resist carrying a digital camera, but a full use of camera in cell phone is made!

Interestingly, the proportion of living, dying and dead pine trees seems the same! A **Principle of Re-generation** is at play: **Shorter a span of a life form, abundance of it is in birth**. In the modern world of human beings, there is a fear of death, and stigma about the dead bodies in the presence of living. Also, there being no shelf space for the dead anywhere, they are 'disposed' off in every culture. However, beauty in the dead pines surpasses, as seen even in the living ones. Of course, the beauty always lies in the eyes of the beholders.

One of the hikers being an oncologist, I asked, "Have you ever seen any beauty in a dying person or in a dead person?" For years, on the average, he has seen 70 dead persons a year. Quickly, he responded, "I have not seen beauty in a dying cancer patient, but once-in-a-while serenity on the face of a dead person, has some beauty about it."

Stories are known about the native Indians in the US—having strong premonitions of their last days on earth. At that hour, they walk out of the teepees, on their own strength, into the forest to free their souls. It must be an awesome sight! In India, young and old people mill around a place where a **Sanyasi** goes into **Samadhi**, a state of union with his/her Supreme. Witnessing the sight is said to be blissful. The place itself becomes holy! My thoughts were ricocheting like this.

We admire beauty in a newly born child, but rarely talk of any beautiful old person. It was all the more amusing to compare beauty in living trees with that of humans. Trees are not dressed up, whereas, humans are always dressed up or down—unless one lives in a nudist colony, or in a jungle tribe far removed from modern civilization. Imagine all humans beings living nudes—like other creatures, then the billion-dollar industry of women lingerie and jewelry will disappear, and so may go down beauty of women over 30!

June 06, 2008

COMMENTS

1. That was a nice rendition of your views and part of our discussions! You certainly have a nice way of capturing your thoughts and a good way of expressing with the gift of your vocabulary. The "serene beauty" of the "Dead and Dying Pine Trees" in comparing with that of "Dead and Dying Human Beings" based on my limited (1976-till date) exposure in my day-to-day life, brings to the limelight the fact that "Anything that breathes will have to die one day". To me, I will say that, in the human beings, while I see the "pain" of death when people are "dying", I have many a times witnessed the "serene beauty", a glow on their face and the peace that overcomes the pain, the minute they have expired. Thank you for allowing me to express my thoughts! **Panju Prithviraj**.

2. "A thing of beauty is a joy forever" . . . This "reflection" was a beautiful one . . . almost poetic. It made me nostalgic. I had been to Mount Charleston last time when I was in Vegas. Thanks.

Life and death are two sides of the same coin . . . " All that lives must die . . . when we accept this reality gracefully, life becomes beautiful . . . there are many things that we can learn from nature . . . provided we have an ear to listen to its sounds and an eye to see its varied beauty . . . **Abraham**

PARADIGM SHIFTS—FROM TENNIS TO MATH

Yesterday, I watched Wimbledon tennis only for the Williams sisters. They were the biggest draw of the tournament, as they steamrolled their opponents in single/double matches. During the all-sister-single final, I observed that the sisters and their parents, also as coaches, have brought a paradigm shift in women tennis. The sisters did not attend any prestigious tennis academy, or college on scholarship. They are street raised and home grown. It is a tough training regimen on the top of their genetic physique that they stand out as thoroughbred tennis players.

Taking Paradigm shifts as a mental exercise, I thought of making a list of paradigm shifts in other aspects of life too. Being a sport aficionado, here are a few more for sports to get it going:

Boxing (Heavyweight); **Muhammad Ali's Rope a Dope**. It was all the genius of Ali that even baffled his ringside trainer during his fight with 'invincible' George Foreman (1974).

Basketball: Michael Jordon's will to win and never to wilt in a game set new benchmarks. He was coached by legendary Dean Smith (North Carolina) and Phil Jackson (Chicago Bulls).

Golf: Tiger Woods was trained by his father. Incidentally, Tiger chose Stanford over UNLV for Golf! His father predicted Tiger's phenomenal success in a book, but the golfers did not believe him.

Mathematics: Invention of **Calculus** independently by Newton and Leibnitz changed the face of mathematics and sciences. One of the many ways to describe Calculus is the **Taming of Infinity**. Come to think of another mathematical invention during the last 100-200 years, nothing else stands out except abstraction of mathematics reaching newer heights. In 1945, mathematical rigor was further pushed by Bourbaki, a group of French pure mathematicians.

Physics: The Special and General Theory of Relativity. It has brought far-reaching consequences due to the study of high speeds near that of light, subatomic particles, and birth of nano-science. The traditional walls in sciences, of physics, chemistry, and biology, are now falling down.

Inventions like airplanes, automobiles, spacecraft and personal computers have changed the courses of mankind. The latest cellular technology has brought internet, video and audio in the palm of a hand. While the geographic distances are eliminated, a person, increasingly confined in the privacy of his/her own 'island', is more vulnerable to mental disorders and external crimes.

Incidentally, the US Independence day on July 4 and Wimbledon have converged together. I venture to say that of all the nations created in the history, **the US is a shining example of a paradigm shift in governments— from monarchies to democracy.** The US went unnoticed for the first 100 years—like the Williams sisters' début 10 years ago. They were ridiculed for braiding white beads into their Afro hair, and dresses they wore. The father was not given any credit for the book he wrote on their training. But the sisters kept wining, and wining so big, that Chris Evert, a woman-tennis legend of the 1970s recently commented, "Williams sisters are too strong to play with women!" History is still in the making!

(July 06, 2008)

COMMENTS

1. One of my biggest hobbies is studying gun history. When I thought of a paradigm shift in the world of handguns, I immediately thought of the **M1911 created by the world's most influential gunsmith, John M. Browning.** Before World War I, the US military used the very inefficient .38 Long Colt. John M. Browning created a gun that would replace the .38 Long Colt, and he presented to the US government the M1911, a single-action, semi-automatic pistol. This pistol changed the US military in that this was an extremely efficient pistol with a high capacity, unsurpassed accuracy, and exceptional stopping power. Almost 100 years later, the M1911 is still used in the US military, and it is the model to which all other handguns are compared. **Elizabeth D'Ercole**

2. Sir, while sitting in the Cox Pavilion yesterday your paradigm shift thought process came to mind. It clicked when the professor from Berkley was talking about the transistor. The transistor was a paradigm shift in the ways of electronics and computers. This simple variation of the vacuum tube gave way to many advancements in the modern world. But what struck me most is that I was sitting among the people that had the means to create a paradigm shift themselves, in fact, that was the intent of this Summit. We were the people charged with the intimate role of propelling this paradigm shift. Many speakers referenced paradigm shifts, like Churchill's switch to a petroleum based economy of which the west followed. Your exercise on paradigm shifts has allowed me to see some things in a different light, and I thank you for that. **SSgt Timothy O'Neill**, 99 CES/CCE 6020 Beale Ave., Nellis AFB, NV 89191

LIVING WITH/OUT WISHES

Since adolescence one starts hearing advices like—you must have goals in life; have a list of things to be accomplished by a certain age, and so on, and on. I have kept journals since college days, but never systematically worked for a set of goals. A story line of a recent movie, *The Bucket List*, is around the **Last Wishes** of two terminal patients. There is no finality about a Wish List, as the number of desires and goals in life is, indeed, infinite. However, it is a big reason to get off the bed in the morning, and do something concrete during a day.

Well, last Sunday, I jogged the historic Golden Gate Bridge of San Francisco (SF). It is only 3.4 miles back and forth. What is a big deal about it? Well, first of all, an achievement of one person may not be even on the radar screen of the other. That is a given fact. A goal is all about you, your feelings for it, your heart pumping for it, and adrenalin rushing at the mere thought of it.

There is a pull about Golden Gate Bridge, as it is related with historic Gold Rush of early 20th century. That is how the state got its name, Golden California. Since 1974, I have driven over the Bridge a dozen times with family and friends, but never parked the car to satisfy this walking urge on it. Now, time 'running out', I sounded my son about it, as he lives 40 miles from it.

Sometimes, a good opportunity presents itself without any planning for it. Then, one must be ready to grab it by the horns. Last Sunday, we, a large party in three cars, spent a family time at the Golden Gate Park and Beach. At the end, I persuaded my son for a walk on the Bridge. The members in the other two cars had no interest in it, so drove back home.

It was 7 PM, and five of us set out for a Bridge walk. The two cables holding the entire suspension bridge (longest in the year 1937) are each more than a mile long, 36" in diameter—packed with nearly 28,000 tiny cables! Warning plates on the Bridge caution, that jumping over it is unlawful and fatal. Who would jump in cold water 260' below? Yet, on the average, one jumps to death every 15 days. Perhaps, the warnings cover the city from liability claims. During my Delhi visit last year, I found the entry to the 12th century, 238' high Qutab Minar closed due to suiciders and terrorists. It is time to open the Minar with high admission fees and surveillance.

Bridge walking was fun. I never saw SF skyline from the Bridge. The bay accentuates the high rises. Alcatraz Island stirred memories of Andaman and Nicobar islands in Indian Ocean—used as a prison for the hardened criminals and Indian freedom fighters during the British occupation of India. Well, I was in my own thoughts—walking, jogging, and feeling energized.

Analyzing the psychology of goals, one cannot do it alone. We are all surrounded by naysayers discouraging from small adventures—like this one; what is there in walking on a bridge? It is no different from walking elsewhere, etc. **Once in a while, it is essential to be surrounded with over-achievers.** With my sister and brother-in-law being ultimate adventurers, my son had to go along. For the fifth one, we were over-achievers, so he tagged along! It is good to have a Wish List. Massage it every now and then. Who knows it may become public markers of life.

(Sep 04, 2008)

COMMENTS

1. Thanks for this story which stimulates my energy dreams. Yes, I want to have more energy and more pep. Oh, you don't believe me??? It's the spurts that get me tired. Hugs, **Dutchie**

Oh, the other day I read that goals have an ending and dreams never end.

2. .... I am at last getting some time to learn some mathematical physics that I didn't get a chance to learn at the right age!! Better late than never. Of course, my particular interests come with a price, viz., not many people who are interested in it, so that the journey is somewhat alone .... So, luckily, between, regular house maintaining chores, grand children, social obligations, my interests in music (listening, singing, playing the violin, harmonium), intellectual interests, I am happily busy. I am sure the same is true with you too. Your earlier reflection on 'wishes' expressed some important truths!! Regards. **RAJA**

SCARS THAT NEVER SCAB

There is really nothing new in any human experience—only, its encounter at the individual level brings semblance of newness. Any human drama of emotions and passions, at every stratum, is perennial. Being recorded at individual level, it is eventually erased and forgotten. Its occurrence becomes new again for the next generations.

This line of thoughts flashed on me yesterday. My wife and I were driving Kay back to her home. We met her at a socio-spiritual gathering two years ago. Sitting in the back seat and being tipsy, she was upset over an incident that happened an hour earlier. Suddenly, it triggered an event in her mind that took place decades ago. In a Sunday Church School, she was slapped so hard that she fell off the chair. Reason: she told the teacher that Mary must have had a relationship with a man before conceiving Jesus. The teacher wanted her to believe that Mary was virgin, and Jesus was the Son of God.

"How old were you to understand the connection between sex and conception?" I asked, while my wife was listening in the passenger seat. When she uttered five years, I said, "How did you get this knowledge at five?" "My father had sexually abused me," she said matter-of-factly. With our Indian puritan upbringing, relatively speaking, both of us were speechless. Kay added, "For years, she wondered—whether she was a virgin or not."

Kay, now a 74 year-old, silver-haired blond, walks straight like a pole. For years, she was a glamorous showgirl in Las Vegas. After retiring, she worked as a comedian in Las Vegas conventions. With beautiful features (Greek heritage), she never had a problem in transitioning from a showroom to a convention floor.

At the gathering, she showed off her stylish sequined pullover that she had knitted. It won her a prize in an Art Fair. Apart from creative hobbies of knitting, sewing and crocheting, she has taken many literature and writing courses at UNLV. She is one of the many non-traditional students who enrich their lives by acquiring knowledge for the sake of it.

For us, Kay's life ran past like a documentary. She was courted by men from Hollywood. Twice, she married, divorced, and sad story of her childlessness.

She lives alone in a big house, drives Mercedes, daily takes a shot of 4 oz. of Vodka, and goes out of the house for her smoke.

What can you say—except, that judging an individual life is not worth it, in the long run? The total picture can never be known. When the conversation resumed from our side, I said that the day is not far-off when pedophilia will be decriminalized in the US, as the minds of the professionals in psychology, social work, and libraries have been working.

My thoughts were bouncing on and off Kay. A story is impactful when heard directly from a person whose scars are still green after 70 years. Freud is damn right about the power of sex, sexuality, and sexual undertones. Libido was Freud's paradigm in life.

(Nov 10, 2008)

COMMENTS

Very provocative statement that " . . . pedophilia will be decriminalized in the US . . . " to me. Investigating the pros and cons will prove very interesting. Thanks, **Dutchie**

PERSONAL COMMENTS

COMMENTATORS AND ANALYSTS EXTRAORDINAIRE

Ten years ago, I started writing **Reflections,** a reincarnation of my lifelong passion of writing letters. The big difference was that that my writings went public—from one to many. I started sharing them with friends and relatives. And from there it went to their friends and relatives, and so on. Four years ago, a student of mine created a blog, but seldom had I posted any. I don't have a website either. It is all emails in a bcc—mode electronically old-fashioned.

I have several mailing lists and I am used to this inefficient mode of communication. I have Facebook and Twitter accounts too, but they too have remained unused. That is my approach to communication. Naturally some write back and give comments. However, at times, a small dialog takes place. It has added clarity and sharpened in my thoughts.

Not all the comments and commentators have been included—only those which are concise and strong. In reflective style of writings, inclusion of some comments adds a new flavor. Initially, I never saved the comment. Also, sometimes, no comments were received. That is why the space following some **Reflections** is blank.

It is not merely a time to thank them, but also share a piece of immortality that this book may bring! When I look at the credentials of these persons I am myself awed and wowed. These comments have come out of their incredible rich backgrounds. I don't think this list can be easily matched. Here are the names in some order:

Raju **Abraham**: Known for six years. English professor—has taught in Baroda/India, Sana/Yemen, and presently in Oman with University of Nizwa, where I was a visiting professor for one semester, Spring 2009.

AK Kundra: Hindu Community leader in Florida. Known for six years, a businessman.

Alex Garza: My son-in-law with Mexican heritage; active in Hispanic community and politics—a successful entrepreneur.

Ashish Saxena, PhD: Distantly related.

BSY/ BS Yadav: Mathematics Professor, known for 15 years. Died two years ago at 78.

Matt Azikhaketh: Physicist by training and became an international expert in nuclear reactor technology in Nevada Test site. After retirement, he studied Greek for the Bible studies. He and his Late wife Connie were our first family friends when we moved to Las Vegas in Aug 1974.

Avnish Bhatnagar: My son, age 43, works at Google. His comments are few, but deep.

Rahul Bhatnagar: Distantly related—physician by training in India. He has an interesting job of medical director of drug safety with a pharmaceutical company. Very astute commentator and analyst of nearly all my *Reflections*—and can refine an issue to a state undistinguishable from the one started with.

Ravi P. Bhatnagar: My first cousin, served in Indian Army as a physician—retired as Colonel.

H S **Bhola**: Emeritus IU professor of education—known since 1971—remains witty and sharp at 80. He often tells me, how exceptional I am, as all math professors that he has known, can hardly write a sentence in English—far from being a literary writer. He continues to write papers and give invited talks.

Ved Bhushan: An 80-year old businessman in Ambala Cantt, India—known since 1980. He still enjoys the pleasures of skin.

Cyriac Chemplavil: Well known lung specialist of Las Vegas, acquainted since 1982.

Gayathri: Knew her as a student in Malaysia during 1998 visit.

Gopal Dass: Retired cardiologist, settled in Las Vegas—has interesting hobbies—known for five years.

Irma **Dutchie**: Our 82—year old neighbor, who lives life with and zing and zest—extremely generous. She is now a member of our extended Bhatnagar family.

Mahesh Gautam: Researcher in Desert Research Institute in Las Vegas. Native of Nepal and has also studied/worked in India and Thailand.

Hardev Singh; Known since 1993, a very successful Industrial executive with a meditative outlook on life.

Hortense Simmons: Retired English Professor; met her in 1992 during my first Malaysian assignment, widely traveled. Died suddenly two years ago from Lou Gehrig disease. She was 68.

S. C. **Gupta**: is a businessman and Arya Samaj leader in Mumbai, India—known for five years.

Aarti Jain: Director/Producer of documentaries on the life of Indians settled in the US. Met her in San Francisco in 2003.

Alok Kumar: Physics professor in NY, PhD IIT, Kanpur—Known for 25 years.

Looy Simonoff: Retired Math professor at UNLV, family friend. Died last year at 83.

Manmohan Singh Arora: Retired Math professor, known for five years.

Panju Prithviraj: Oncologist working out from Cleveland and Las Vegas

Prafulla Raval: Chemistry PhD, known for 40 years since IU days.

Ranjana Kumar: Director of an Adult Day Care Center in Charlotte, NC—know since 1977.

Satyam **Moorty**: Emeritus English professor, Southern Utah University—known since 1978.

Sandeep Shrivastav: Just finishing his MD, known for five years

Sarojini Menon: PhD psychology, known for 29 years since Malaysian days.

Sham Narula: An octogenarian retired engineer—active in senior activities in Washington DC area.

Surendra Singh: Biology professor at Newman University; still engaged at 78.

Anjali Nigam: My daughter's daughter who has been reading, commenting, editing and proofing most of my Reflections ever since. Currently, she is doing Doctorate in occupational therapy from Washington University, St. Louis.

R S **Nigam**: Retired Professor of Commerce and Director of Delhi School of Economics—known for 25 years.

Rene Riendero: Life explorer and realtor. Wrote a book on her experiences of visiting India. It encouraged her to become a writer.

Gurdev Singh: 70+ year old Gandhian and a long-time associate of Subbarao—retired professor of Punjabi.

Harpreet Singh: A rare combination of computer science, finance, active spirituality, and creative writing—always exploring and stretching his limits. He is 36 years old and known for 13 years through his parents first.

Inder Singh: Age 74, a pioneer amongst the first generation of Indians in the US, community leader and social activist in several organizations. Currently, president of GOPIO (Global Organization of Persons of India Origin). Lives in LA and known for 15 years.

Subhash Sood: Physician by training in India, UK and USA. He never practiced for profit, though studied other systems of medicine too— eccentric to a certain degree. However, he was deeply drawn into by Scientology—established the first center in India, and translated several scientology books from English into Hindi. He died in 2007 at age 74—in a 100—year old, now dilapidated, mansion in which he was born, as the only son of a physician, in Ambala Cant. He was my most avid reader and friend for over 25 years.

E. **Sooriamurthy**: Retired physics professor Madurai University, India— known since 1968—our common days at IU. His son, Raja, computer science professor at Carnegie Mellon is an avid reader of my Reflections too.